Manag

Rajvinder Kandola is a chartered occupational psychologist and founding partner of Pearn Kandola. After gaining a B.Sc. (Econ.) in Psychology, an MA in Occupational Psychology and a Ph.D. examining the fair use of tests, he began professional work in equal opportunities and diversity. His 16 years' experience in these fields has involved research, training and consultancy. He was the first chair of the British Psychological Society's standing committee on the promotion of equal opportunities and a member of Sir Robin Butler's panel of inquiry into equal opportunities in the senior levels of the Civil Service.

Johanna Fullerton, who holds a B.Sc. in Psychology and an M.Sc. in Occupational Psychology, has worked with Pearn Kandola for five years, specialising in managing diversity, and is now based in the Dublin office. She has been involved in several major assignments such as conducting attitude surveys into diversity, evaluating and auditing organisations and conducting diversity training.

Managing the Mosaic
Diversity in action

Rajvinder Kandola

and

Johanna Fullerton

INSTITUTE OF PERSONNEL
AND DEVELOPMENT

First published in 1994
Reprinted 1996

Typeset by The Comp-Room, Aylesbury
Printed in Great Britain by
The Cromwell Press, Wiltshire

British Library Cataloguing in Publication Data
A catalogue record for this book is available from the
British Library

ISBN 0-85292-556-5

The views expressed in this book are the authors' own and
may not necessarily reflect those of the IPD.

**INSTITUTE OF PERSONNEL
AND DEVELOPMENT**

IPD House, Camp Road, London SW19 4UX
Tel: 0181 971 9000 Fax: 0181 263 3333
Registered office as above. Registered Charity No. 1038333
A company limited by guarantee. Registered in England No. 2931892

 **Contents**

Acknowledgements   vi

 1. Introduction   1
 2. The Diversity Mosaic   6
 3. The Population Mosaic   21
 4. The Benefits Mosaic   32
 5. Diversity Initiatives   54
 6. A Model for Managing Diversity   74
 7. A Diversity Competence: the Role of the Individual   102
 8. Gaining Diversity in Your Processes   116
 9. Positive Action and Targets: The Pieces That Do Not Fit   131
10. MOSAIC: Our Vision of the Diversity-Oriented
    Organisation   150
11. The Final Piece: Completing the Picture   173

Appendix   178
References   180
Index   190

Acknowledgements

This book could not have been completed without the support and hard work at Pearn Kandola of Stephanie Heath, to whom we are immensely grateful. We would also like to thank Chris Mulrooney, Candida Watts and Sandra Macleod for their help.

In addition we would like to thank Professor Ivan Robertson at UMIST and Yasmin Ahmed at Pearn Kandola for their assistance on the validated model of diversity.

We are also very grateful to Phil Wills, Director of Compensation and Benefits at International Distillers and Vintners for allowing us to use IDV as a case study, and to Matthew Reisz, our editor at IPD, for his confidence in us and his patience.

Finally we would like to thank all the people who completed questionnaires as part of our research. We hope you find it was worthwhile.

1

Introduction

The term 'managing diversity' is one that is going to be heard much more over the next few years. Its use is already widespread in the USA and has been so since 1987, when a highly influential book, entitled *Workforce 2000* (Johnston and Packer 1987) was produced by the Hudson Institute, which showed how the population of America was going to be changing over the next decade. Amongst some of the startling facts it presented was that white males would be a minority of new entrants to the labour force by the year 2000. This made many academics and business people, particularly those in the human resource field, take notice of the changing demographic situation and consider its effects. In 1990 the *Harvard Business Review* published an article by R. R. Thomas entitled 'From affirmative action to affirming diversity'. This explored the fundamental principles on which much equal opportunities work is based and presented a different way forward in the shape of managing diversity.

Since then there has been a plethora of articles and books written on the subject, nearly all of them American. In the UK we have seen an increasing use of the term 'managing diversity' but as yet we have come across few attempts to define and interpret this concept.

In this book, therefore, we are attempting to define what managing diversity means and how it should be applied strategically within organisations. It is an amalgamation of information from at least three sources. First, it is based on a comprehensive review of the relevant diversity literature. Second, it contains original research data based on our survey of 285 organisations in the UK. This research identified the diversity initiatives being undertaken and, more importantly, the perceived effectiveness of these initiatives. Our research also went on to examine and validate a strategic implementation model of diversity. This represents, we believe, the first *validated* model of diversity. Third, it is based on our own

experience of many years' work in organisations on both equal
opportunities and managing diversity issues. In our work we have
come across many examples of good practice and some of those are
contained within this book. However, we have also seen some of
the mistakes that organisations have made and that are too often
ignored, which is a great shame as they provide an opportunity to
learn from the mistakes of the past in order to build more effective
strategies for the future. Some of these mistakes are included
within this book.

Apart from defining diversity, we are also attempting to strip
away much of the rhetoric that surrounds it. We feel this is important as organisations will only actively manage diversity if they can
see the benefits clearly without having them dressed up. Our review
of the diversity literature has led us to the conclusion that some of
the benefits claimed for managing diversity have been exaggerated.
We hope that by removing some of the more extravagant claims
and promises that have been made for diversity we can identify the
real and actual benefits that will accrue to an organisation by
adopting the approaches we are putting forward.

Managing diversity, we believe, offers great potential for organisations in enabling them to make better use of all their employees.
But it needs a vision that is clear-sighted and free of rhetoric, coupled
with a determination to make the vision a reality. We hope this
book not only provides a starting-point for a re-evaluation of the
work that has been done in the name of equal opportunities but also
a chance to make a new start. We hope that we will stimulate as
well as educate, and be provocative as well as informative.

Throughout the book we have referred to examples that we have
come across in the literature or in our own experience. Many of
these examples come from organisations in the USA who have a
longer track record in these issues than organisations in the UK.
However, one UK organisation that has begun in the past few years
to examine diversity is International Distillers and Vintners. We are
very grateful to IDV, one of the world's largest drinks companies
and part of Grand Metropolitan, for access to their information.
IDV is probably best known for brands such as Cinzano, J&B
Whisky, Bailey's, Piat d'Or, Metaxa and Smirnoff (to name but a

few) and operates in over 60 different countries. Given the variety of its products, people and operations, IDV has recognised that diversity is an issue it must address. We have used IDV as an example at several points during the book and written up its work more extensively in Chapter 6. We are particularly grateful for their co-operation and especially to Phil Wills, the champion of diversity within IDV.

The structure of the book: a brief overview

Chapter 2   The diversity mosaic

The changing face of equal opportunities is examined, and in par-ticular the emphasis now being placed on the business case, the increased profile given to ethical behaviour in the workplace, and changes in the legislation. All of these issues together have stimu-lated the need for a more overarching, all-encompassing approach: this is where diversity has a part to play.

Chapter 3   The population mosaic

The working population of the UK is more diverse today than it has ever been. With more women coming into the labour market, more ethnic minorities and an ageing population, organisations are faced with a diversity within their workforce unheard of before. The changes taking place are described in this chapter.

Chapter 4   The benefits mosaic

A critical examination is undertaken of the literature relating to the benefits of managing a diverse workforce. The claims that have been made are examined to see the extent to which they are sup-ported and substantiated by concrete evidence. We present those claims which we feel are proven benefits and can be supported,

those benefits which are debatable and, finally, we look at the indirect
benefits which to some extent may not be possible to measure. The
intention is to identify the true, measurable benefits that can be
attributed to diversity in order to build a solid foundation for work
in the future.

Chapter 5   Diversity initiatives

We undertook a survey of 285 organisations within the UK asking
them about the type of initiatives that they have undertaken in the
diversity field. The results of this survey, looking in particular at
those initiatives which work and those which do not appear to
work, are presented here. The chapter also examines the rationale
for taking action and how the actions are evaluated and monitored.

Chapter 6   A model for managing diversity

Many authors have put forward their own strategic models for managing a diverse workforce; these are critically examined for their
practicality and logic. Based on a synthesis of these, our own
strategic implementation model is put forward together with data
representing our attempt to validate it. We believe this is the first
validated model of a diversity strategy to have been developed.

Chapter 7   A diversity competence: the role of the individual

In this chapter we look at the role of individual managers in managing a diverse workforce. This is preceded by a discussion of
stereotyping and how this can affect decisions that managers make
in the workforce. We also look at the dangers of some of the diversity approaches and how they can create rather than remove stereotypes. Finally, some actions are presented that individual managers
can take in order to improve their skills in managing a diverse
workforce.

Chapter 8   Gaining diversity in your processes

We examine some key processes and what organisations can do to
ensure that they are objective, effective and fair. In particular we
look at recruitment, selection, induction and appraisal. If these
processes are not working effectively and fairly then there is little
chance that an organisation can ever hope to claim it is managing
diversity effectively.

Chapter 9   Positive action and targets: the pieces that do not fit

Managing diversity is a different concept from equal opportunities,
particularly in its focus on individuals rather than groups. In this
chapter some of the implications for this focus are explored particularly in relation to positive action, or affirmative action as it is
sometimes known, and targets. We believe that such approaches
do not fit in with a managing diversity approach and need to be
rethought if an organisation truly wishes to become diversity-
oriented.

Chapter 10   Mosaic: our vision of the diversity-oriented organisation

We take a leap into the future and attempt to define our vision of
the diversity-oriented organisation, what it would look like and the
features it would have.

Chapter 11   The final piece: completing the picture

The key points of the book are reiterated and some final observa-
tions are made.

2

The Diversity Mosaic

Managing diversity means different things to different people. It can mean integrating different parts of an organisation to enable them to work together (eg Goold and Campbell 1987; Calori 1988); it can relate to the issue of national cultures within a multinational organisation (eg Hofstede 1984; Trompenaars 1993; Bartlett and Ghoshal 1989; Phillips 1992); it can also refer to the development of equal opportunities. It is on this third area that our book will concentrate: the evolution and transformation of equal opportunities into managing diversity.

In this chapter the following issues will be addressed:

- defining what managing diversity is and how it differs from equal opportunities
- providing some of the reasons behind much of the work on managing diversity.

Managing diversity – definitions

This section gives different definitions of managing diversity together with our own definition, which not only attempts to capture the essential themes but will also provide the basis for our ideas throughout the book. The section then goes on to address how managing diversity differs from conventional concepts of equal opportunities.

Definitions

Many definitions of managing diversity have been produced; Table 2.1 provides a sample of them. From these it is possible to identify some key features, for example:

6

Table 2.1
Definitions of diversity

- 'Understanding that there are differences among employees and that these differences, if properly managed, are an asset to work being done more efficiently and effectively. Examples of diversity factors are race, culture, ethnicity, gender, age, a disability, and work experience.' Bartz, Hillman, Lehrer and Mayhugh (1990: 321).
- 'The concept of managing diversity is inclusive – diversity includes white males. Managing diversity does not mean that white males are managing women and minorities, but rather that all managers are managing all employees. The objective becomes that of creating an environment that taps the potential of all employees without any group being advantaged by irrelevant classification or accident of birth.' Hammond and Kleiner (1992: 7).
- 'People are different from one another in many ways – in age, gender, education, values, physical ability, mental capacity, personality, experiences, culture and the way each approaches work. Gaining the diversity advantage means acknowledging, understanding, and appreciating these differences and developing a workplace that enhances their value – by being flexible enough to meet needs and preferences – to create a motivating and rewarding environment.' Jamieson and O'Mara (1991: 3–4).
- Employers must 'seek out all available strategies that will bring them the talent they need in the years to come. One such strategy is to understand our own cultural filters and to accept differences in people so that each person is treated and valued as a unique individual.' Kennedy and Everest (1991: 50).
- 'Diversity refers to much more than skin colour and gender. It can encompass age, race, religious affiliation, economic class, military experience and sexual orientation.' Galagan (1991: 41).
- 'Cultural diversity creates an environment in which individual differences are evident, different means to an end are respected, and the talent and attributes of people from different backgrounds and heritages are fully valued, utilised and developed. Such an environment, we believe, can achieve superior business results.' Greenslade (1991: 78).
- Managing diversity 'means enabling every member of your workforce to perform to his or her potential. It means getting from employees, first, everything we have a right to expect, and, second, if we do it well – everything they have to give.' R. R. Thomas (1990: 112).

- Diversity and differences between people can, and should, if managed effectively, add value to the organisation.
- Diversity includes virtually all ways in which people differ, not just the more obvious ones of gender, ethnicity and disability.
- Diversity has as its primary concern organisational culture and the working environment.

Bearing these definitions in mind, plus the key philosophical bases underlying the concepts, we have produced our working definition which will form the central theme for the discussions in this book.

> **The basic concept of managing diversity accepts that the workforce consists of a diverse population of people. The diversity consists of visible and non-visible differences which will include factors such as sex, age, background, race, disability, personality and workstyle. It is founded on the premiss that harnessing these differences will create a productive environment in which everybody feels valued, where their talents are being fully utilised and in which organisational goals are met.**

This definition contrasts with the assimilation theories of the 1960s and 1970s, which conceived of organisations and of society generally as being a melting-pot. The problem with these theories, according to Nkomo (1991), is they led to the belief that assimilation was a one-way process that required minorities to adopt the norms and practices of the majority. If a group was not seen to have assimilated it was assumed the problem lay within that group rather than in the dominant culture.

Managing diversity, if it has an overriding image of an organisation, sees it as a mosaic. Differences come together to create a whole organisation in much the same way that single pieces of a mosaic come together to create a pattern. Each piece is acknowledged, accepted and has a place in the whole structure.

If managing diversity is to be seen as a new concept, however, the set of ideas that represented the body of conventional wisdom within the equal opportunities field must, by definition, change. If it does not, then managing diversity will merely be used as a convenient and perhaps more accessible label for the ideas currently under the heading of equal opportunities. Several authors see managing diversity as different from equal opportunities in a number of ways (Hall and Parker 1993; Ross and Schneider 1992; Jamieson and O'Mara 1991; Thomas 1990; Dickson 1992):

- *First, managing diversity is not just about concentrating on issues of discrimination, but about ensuring that all people maximise their potential and their contribution to the organisation.* One of the starting-points for many equal opportunities policies is to ensure that there is no unlawful discrimination taking place (see Chapter 5, which provides more data on this). The impetus is primarily legal and perhaps rather defensive ie organisations want to keep within the law. Consequently their priorities will naturally be on those areas covered by the anti-discrimination legislation, namely race, gender and, in Northern Ireland, religion. But managing diversity has a much more positive message: that valuing people and enabling them to work to their full potential will make the workplace more inviting and will benefit the long-term vitality and profitability of the organisation.
- *Second, it is a concept that embraces a broad range of people.* Equal opportunities is typically perceived as about and for women, ethnic minorities and disabled people. If you do not fit into any one or more of these categories, then equal opportunities may not be championing your cause. In essence, managing diversity should not exclude anyone – even white, middle-class males.

  Many of those involved in equal opportunities will claim, with some justification, that their work has not been focused exclusively on these groups. However, there can be little doubt that the *perception* of equal opportunities is that it is group-focused. Furthermore, when one examines the actions that organisations take they are invariably, if not exclusively, centred on one or more of those groups.
- *Third, managing diversity concentrates on movement within the*

organisation, the culture of the organisation, and the meeting of business objectives. This means, therefore, that there must be a perceived benefit in taking any action and that the action should be evaluated to see if the benefits are actually realised. The most obvious areas are for example turnover rates of women and men; return rates of women after pregnancy; promotion ratios of different groups who entered the organisation at the same time; access issues for people with a disability. By addressing issues such as these properly, the organisation will be forced to look at the systems and policies it has in place, and the attitudes and skills of the workforce generally and of managers in particular. In overall terms, however, the organisation wishes to have high-quality human resource processes in place to enable people to perform to their highest potential. Managing diversity is not just about looking at the numbers of different groups employed.

- *Fourth, equal opportunities was often seen as something that concerned mainly personnel and human resource practitioners. Managing diversity, however, is seen as being the concern of all employees, especially managers, within an organisation.* Responsibility lies with all employees, but managers have a crucial part to play. This in turn means making them more accountable for the manner in which they manage their staff. They need to be developed appropriately to ensure they have the skills to manage a diverse workforce (an issue that is covered more comprehensively in Chapter 7).

- *Fifth, managing diversity differs from equal opportunities in its lack of reliance upon positive action or, as it is sometimes referred to, affirmative action.* (Positive action or affirmative action is where organisations take special initiatives to redress perceived gender or ethnic imbalances in the workforce eg by providing special training for women and minorities.) Some authors have asserted strongly that managing diversity offers an alternative to affirmative action approaches. According to Harisis and Kleiner (1993) affirmative action was based on the following premisses:
  - adult, white males constitute what is referred to as the business mainstream

- discrimination and prejudice keep women and minorities out of certain sectors of the job market and they should be allowed in
- as a matter of public policy and common decency
- legal and social pressures are needed to bring about the change.

They believe this is no longer considered appropriate. To maintain competitiveness, organisations must recruit, develop and promote on the basis of competence rather than group membership. Some (eg Dickson 1992; Thomas 1990; Jamieson and O'Mara 1991) have argued that affirmative action needs to be reviewed in the light of managing diversity. Their arguments could be taken a step further. If managing diversity is about individuals and their contribution to an organisation rather than about groups, it is contradictory to provide training and other opportunities based solely on people's perceived group membership. (This issue is discussed in more depth in Chapter 9.)

Our view is that diversity has to be considered as something different from equal opportunities and not as merely a new label for an old concept.

We also feel that the time is ripe for a reconsideration of the conventional approaches to equal opportunities. Equal opportunities, it is often said, is about change. It is rather ironic, therefore, to find that this slogan is not inherent in the concept of equal opportunities itself. The body of ideas representing conventional wisdom in equal opportunities has not changed in possibly the last 15 years.

For example, the ideas produced by Wainwright (1979) are little different from those provided 10 years later by Straw (1989). As further evidence, the Codes of Practice produced in the UK by the Commission for Racial Equality (1984) and the Equal Opportunities Commission (1985) have not been revised since they were written – although we recognise that the government may have something to do with that. And yet, during this time, organisations have been forced into considerable change. It is only right, therefore, that the ideas which have formed the structure and background of much thinking on equal opportunities should also be reviewed and re-evaluated.

Table 2.2 shows an organisational response to diversity. It provides the definition and explanatory guide to diversity within International Distillers and Vintners (IDV). This was produced as an internal document to explain the concept to human resource people at first and then for use with other managers. It was felt that unless there was clarity about the concept and its application, there was a high probability it would be misunderstood.

Table 2.2
How IDV define diversity

1.   What does it mean to 'value diversity'?
1.1   Valuing diversity means valuing the differences between people and the ways in which those differences can contribute to a richer, more creative and more productive business environment, which is closer to our many different customers world-wide.
1.2   Valuing diversity means valuing the qualities that different people bring to their jobs, to the resolution of problems and to the development of business opportunities – rather than judging people and ideas by the extent to which they conform to our existing values or personal preferences.
2.   What does diversity cover?
Diversity results from differences in gender, ethnic or national origin, religion, age, physical or mental capabilities, marital status, sexual preference, social background, organisational role and many other factors which cause people to have different perspectives on the same set of facts or issues.
3.   What does 'managing diversity' mean?
'Managing diversity' is about managing people who are not like you, and who do not necessarily aspire to be like you. It is about having the management skill to allow their different perspectives and views to improve the quality of your decisions.
4.   Is 'diversity' the same as 'equal opportunities'?
Diversity is a concept which recognises the benefits to be gained from differences. 'Equal Opportunities' has traditionally been a concept which sought to legislate against discrimination.
The two concepts have the following characteristics:

EQUAL OPPORTUNITY	vs.	DIVERSITY

EQUAL OPPORTUNITY	DIVERSITY
– externally initiated	– internally initiated
– legally driven	– business-needs driven
– quantitative focus *(ie improving the numbers)*	– qualitative focus *(ie improving the environment)*
– problem-focused	– opportunity-focused
– assumes assimilation	– assumes pluralism
– reactive	– proactive
– race, gender and disability	– all differences

5. **What is diversity *not* about?**

   – It is not about reducing standards.
   – It is not about removing our prejudices. It is about recognising they exist and then questioning them before we act.
   – It is not a distraction from more important business issues. Like Quality it is a standard by which our business performance is measured.
   – It is not about positive discrimination. It is about positive action.
   – It is not just about language and political correctness.

The equality mosaic: the changing face of equal opportunities

In recent years, probably since the onset of the recession in the early 1990s, there have been subtle, but nevertheless significant, shifts of emphasis in the way equal opportunities are viewed and consequently implemented. These include:

- a more overt emphasis on the business case
- an increasing amount of research showing the discrimination and harassment faced by a wide range of groups in society generally and in the workplace in particular
- concern about ethics and ethical business conduct and a recognition that equal opportunities is an important and integral part of this debate.

Focus on the business case

According to Donaldson (1993) the recession has forced organisations to examine more closely the actions they are taking and the value of doing them. One indicator of the changes is that in local authorities the number of race units fell from 34 in 1991 to 18 in 1993. Similarly, the number of women's units has fallen from 50 in 1989 to 38 in 1993.

Ann Rennie, who at the time was head of the equal opportunities unit in the National Westminster Bank, is quoted in Donaldson (1993). The bank and her unit had moved their focus from 'quantity to quality issues' (Donaldson 1993: 12). The actions and initiatives that were implemented successfully were those which could be supported by a strong business case, for example homeworking or teleworking. The case for working in this way was that it was *demonstrably* better for the individuals *and* for the bank. As Rennie stated: 'The board was won over by the irrefutable logic that for certain types of jobs, working in new ways was more cost-effective' (Donaldson 1993: 12).

The bank's perspective on equal opportunities was summed up by Lord Alexander, its chief executive: 'The issue of equal opportunities is very much a business one. Using everyone's talents to the full, and developing an environment where all employees are given an equal opportunity to succeed, based on ability, can only lead to a stronger, fitter organisation' (Donaldson 1993: 12).

Issues faced by other groups

More and more research evidence is being published which shows what we have always known: that discrimination and harassment can be carried out on many grounds apart from those of race and gender; that detrimental stereotypes and assumptions can affect the career prospects of more than just ethnic minorities and women; and that unfair practices within organisations will impact in more ways than just on the areas of sex and ethnicity. Organisations have focused on these issues because the legislation exists in these areas. Focusing on the areas that legislators present to us may be helpful in some ways, but it could also lead to a narrowing of the areas of concern: for example, pressure from the European Union (EU) will probably mean that more attention will focus on issues to do with gender rather than race over the next few years. The effects of this can already be seen within the UK, where more attention is being given and more progress is expected to be made in sex equality than any other area (see Chapter 5).

And yet, more and more research shows us the different reasons for discrimination within the workplace. Table 2.3 provides some examples of recent research.

Table 2.3
Discrimination faced by groups

Gays and lesbians

- 22 per cent had experienced discrimination when applying for jobs.
- 24 per cent had experienced discrimination in promotion.
- 18 per cent had faced attempted dismissal or had been dismissed because they were known or suspected to be gay.
- 48 per cent had been harassed because of their sexuality.
- The report called for sexual orientation to be included in equal opportunities and harassment policies.

(Stonewall 1993)

Disability

- Survey made of 1,855 randomly chosen organisations and 351 chosen for their good practice.
- Only one in 20 organisations met or came close to meeting the legal quota.
- Stereotypical views held of disabled people.
- 56 per cent expressed concern about disabled people's ability to do the job and about their productivity.
- Three-quarters of those employing disabled people had experienced no difficulties.
- 42 per cent of organisations without disabled employees anticipated additional costs.
- Half of employers with disabled employees had incurred no extra costs.

(Honey, Meager and Williams 1993)

Age

- European Union study made of age discrimination.
- Increasing numbers of workers of 50 years of age or older are 'persuaded' to leave work through redundancy (compulsory or voluntary) or early retirement.
- In most countries recruitment discrimination starts at age 40.
- Age discrimination considered to be 'rife'.

(Eurolink Age 1993)

Other areas of concern include equal opportunities for part-time workers, members of trade unions and religious groups, regarding dress worn to work, and so on. All these issues have been addressed by research or been tested in industrial tribunals. However, and perhaps inevitably, either of these examines equality from their own perspective. For example, the research may have been carried out by a lobby group who want the data to support their calls for organisations to tackle the issues that are of special concern to them, or someone may have brought a tribunal case where they want their particular grievance dealt with.

Each piece of research has its own set of recommendations, usually along the lines that governments need to bring in specific and additional anti-discrimination legislation and that organisations need specific policies to tackle the problems.

We do not feel that it is either effective or efficient for organisations to operate by producing policies on an *ad hoc* basis without having an overall framework within which they are positioned. A statement, vision and policy on managing diversity would, we feel, provide that framework.

The concern about ethical conduct at work

There has been increasing concern in recent years over the ethical conduct of business. Some authors have identified the links between ethical conduct of people at work and the issues of equality and diversity. For example, Rennie (1993: 56) feels that 'it may be more helpful to eschew the use of the term "equal opportunities" altogether. Instead, in order to understand the ethical operations of personnel policies and practices at work, it might be preferable to focus on the following concepts:

- fulfilment of human potential at work
- preservation of human dignity at work and
- promotion of fair treatment.'

This redefinition of equal opportunities is indeed very similar to our definition of managing diversity.

Paine (1994) takes the argument further and sees ethics as a corporate as well as a personal issue, relating directly to integrity. As she states: 'From the perspective of integrity, the task of ethics management is to define and give life to an organisation's guiding values, to create an environment that supports ethically sound behaviour, and to instil a sense of shared accountability among employees' (Paine 1994: 111). She then goes on to describe several integrity initiatives and strategies. These have varied within organisations: 'Some companies focus on the core values of integrity that reflect basic social obligations, such as respect for the rights of others, honesty, fair dealing, and obedience to the law. Other companies emphasize aspirations – values that are ethically desirable but not necessarily morally obligatory – such as good service to customers, a commitment to diversity, and involvement in the community' (Paine 1994: 111–12).

This concern over ethical standards of behaviour is most clearly seen in recent developments relating to sexual harassment. The European Union (EU) code of practice on the issue considers it from the angle of employees' dignity, as its title shows: 'The Protection of the Dignity of Men and Women at Work.' Similarly, in a recent case of sexual harassment in a US-owned but London-based merchant bank, much of the press attention focused on the bank's high ethical standards, and it was the departure from these standards that led to the resignations of three highly-paid dealers. The *Financial Times* (24 April 1994) reported a bank spokesman as saying that 'the bank had a strict policy on conduct which it expected its employees to follow. Individuals who were repeatedly seen to breach this code would be asked to do the "appropriate thing" '. Will Hutton in the *Guardian* (28 April 1994) argued that the sacking of the three investment bankers 'was as much an economic as social act; an investment in creating a culture that is neutral to men and women and so allowing the firm to better use its female resources'.

The implication of the current work on ethical behaviour and organisational integrity is that if an organisation is truly concerned about these issues then it must logically be concerned about the respect and dignity with which people are treated at work.

The mosaic of legislation

Although it is not the intention of this book to provide detailed information on the provisions of the anti-discrimination legislation, it is nevertheless something that managers in organisations need to be aware of. Across the EU many issues are now covered by anti-discrimination legislation although the laws do not necessarily apply in all of the countries. Sex discrimination legislation of some sort exists in every EU country. There is specific race discrimination legislation in Great Britain and the Netherlands, and religious discrimination legislation in Northern Ireland. In France it is unlawful to use age criteria in recruiting and selecting people.

There are two members of the EU – France and the Netherlands – that have anti-discrimination legislation relating to the employment of gay men and lesbians. A French law enacted on 25 July 1985 inserted the words 'sex', 'family situation' and '*moeurs*' (which can be roughly translated as morals, habits, lifestyle, including sexual orientation) into most of the anti-discrimination provisions of the Penal Code, the Code of Criminal Procedure and the Code of Labour. In France, therefore, it is unlawful for an employer to dismiss or not to employ someone because of his or her *moeurs*, which covers sexual orientation. In the Netherlands a law enacted on 14 November 1991 amended the anti-discrimination provisions of the Penal Code so as to cover discrimination on the basis of heterosexual or homosexual orientation.

We note these different pieces of anti-discrimination legislation because as we move towards greater harmonisation of standards across Europe organisations may well have to take all these legal factors into account. Furthermore, organisations working across Europe will obviously need to take all the relevant legislation into account. It would seem ridiculous for a pan-European organisation to allow certain forms of unfair discrimination to take place in some of their operations and to clamp down on it in others. The mosaic of anti-discrimination legislation will mean organisations applying the same standards across all their sites.

Key points

- Managing diversity has come to mean many things, but the area we are concentrating on in this book is managing diversity as an evolutionary step in the implementation of equal opportunities.
- Our working definition of managing diversity is as follows:
  The basic concept of managing diversity accepts that the workforce consists of a diverse population of people. The diversity consists of visible and non-visible differences which will include sex, age, background, race, disability, personality and workstyle. It is founded on the premiss that harnessing these differences will create a productive environment in which everybody feels valued, where their talents are being fully utilised, and in which organisational goals are met.
- Diversity, we feel, differs from equal opportunities in several key ways:
  - Managing diversity is not just about concentrating on issues of discrimination, but about ensuring that all people maximise their potential and their contribution to the organisation.
  - It embraces a broad range of people.
  - It concentrates on issues of movement within the organisation, the culture of the organisation, and the meeting of business objectives.
  - Equal opportunities was often seen as the concern mainly of personnel and human resource practitioners. Managing

diversity, however, is seen as the concern of all employees, especially managers, within an organisation.
- Managing diversity does not rely upon positive action or, as it is sometimes referred to, affirmative action.
- Equal opportunities has changed in recent years. For example:
  - There is more concern for the business case.
  - Increasing amounts of research show discrimination against more groups than just those covered by the legislation.
  - Increasingly it is being linked to other issues in the workplace, such as ethical conduct. If our contention is correct, then there should be a correlation between those organisations with strong ethical stances and the managing of diversity.
  However, organisations cannot afford to respond to each of these as separate issues. A more coherent, overarching and linking theme is needed, and we believe that managing diversity provides it.
- Finally, as standards become harmonised across Europe it is important to recognise that anti-discrimination legislation covers different subjects in different countries. By adopting a diversity-oriented approach organisations can prepare themselves for any eventuality.

3

⊞ The Population Mosaic

One of the most compelling reasons given by many authors why organisations have to manage diversity is the population changes taking place, particularly in the USA and Western Europe. This chapter examines those changes.

Demographic changes in the UK

Ethnic minorities

The first analysis of the national ethnic minority settlement pattern, drawn from the 1991 census, has been published. Several demographic changes among ethnic minorities are anticipated which are expected to have an impact on organisations.

The national picture. The overall picture according to the Centre for Research in Ethnic Relations (CRER 1993) is as follows (see Table 3.1):

- 5.5 per cent of the population of Great Britain is of ethnic minority origin. The total population is just under 54.9 million, of which the total ethnic minority is just over 3 million. Of these approximately half were born in Britain.
- Nearly half of the ethnic total is made up of people of South Asian origin representing 2.7 per cent of the total British population, with Indians accounting for 1.5 per cent and Pakistanis about 1 per cent.
- Afro-Caribbean people comprise the second largest minority group, representing 1.6 per cent of the population.
- 'Chinese and others' is also a substantial group, representing 1.2 per cent of the total population.

- Members of ethnic minority groups are younger on average than the white population. Although ethnic minorities form 5.5 per cent of the total population, they comprise 9.2 per cent of those aged between 0–4 years, 9 per cent of those between 5–21, 6.9 per cent of those between 16–24 years and 6.1 per cent of those between 25–44 years.
- 16 per cent of the population as a whole is over 65 years of age, but only just over 3 per cent of the ethnic minority population falls within this age group.

Table 3.1

Ethnic group composition of the population in 1991 (%)

Ethnic Group	Great Britain	England & Wales	England	Wales	Scotland
White	94.5	94.1	93.8	98.5	98.7
Ethnic minorities	5.5	6.0	6.3	1.4	1.4
Black	1.6	1.8	1.9	0.3	0.1
Black Caribbean	0.9	1.0	1.1	0.1	0.0
Black African	0.4	0.4	0.4	0.1	0.0
Black other	0.3	0.4	0.4	0.1	0.0
South Asian	2.7	2.9	3.0	0.6	0.6
Indian	1.5	1.7	1.8	0.2	0.2
Pakistani	0.9	0.9	1.0	0.2	0.4
Bangladeshi	0.3	0.3	0.3	0.1	0.0
Chinese & others	1.2	1.2	1.3	0.6	0.5
Chinese	0.3	0.3	0.3	0.2	0.2
Other-Asian	0.4	0.4	0.4	0.1	0.1
Other-other	0.5	0.6	0.6	0.3	0.2
Total Population (000s)	54,860	49,861	47,026	2,835	4,998

Regional patterns.   There are, however, some interesting regional variations. For example:

- Greater London accounts for 44.8 per cent of Great Britain's ethnic minority population, though it accounts for only 10.3 per cent of the white population.

- The other main concentration of ethnic minority population is in the West Midlands, which accounts for 14.6 per cent of the overall population. It is particularly concentrated in the former metropolitan county centred on Birmingham: only 9 per cent of the white population is located there.
- Elsewhere, West Yorkshire and Greater Manchester display the highest relative concentrations of people from ethnic minorities. Black people are strongly represented in the metropolitan counties of the North West, and Yorkshire and Humberside.
- By contrast, South Asians are more widely distributed, with major concentrations in the East Midlands, Yorkshire and Humberside, and the North West.

The key findings of the Labour Force Survey (Sly 1994) identified the following in relation to ethnic minorities:

- Economic activity rates for people of working age were highest for the white population (79 per cent) and for those of black origin (73 per cent) and lowest for people of Pakistani/Bangladeshi origin (43 per cent).
- Self-employment was more common (25 per cent) among working men of Indian or Pakistani/Bangladeshi origin than in the corresponding white population (16 per cent).
- Over half of ethnic minority men and nearly two-thirds of those of Indian origin were in non-manual (mainly managerial, technical and professional) occupations, compared with half of men in the white group.
- Among women of working age economic activity rates were highest in the white population (72 per cent) and lowest for those of Pakistani or Bangladeshi origin (25 per cent).
- Working women from ethnic minority groups were less likely to work as part-time employees (25 per cent) than their white counterparts (40 per cent).
- In 1992 and 1993 unemployment rates for people of ethnic minority origin were about double those for the white population, and this difference applied after age, sex and level of qualification were taken into account.

- Among young people aged 16–24 participation in the labour market was much lower for the ethnic minority groups (52 per cent overall). This is largely accounted for by the higher percentage within these groups who are students.
- Qualification levels attained by 16–24-year-olds from most ethnic minority groups were very similar to those of young white people, though almost half of the Pakistani/Bangladeshi group had no qualifications, compared with less than one-fifth of the white population. People of Indian origin were the most likely to have higher-level qualifications.

People with disabilities

Martin, Meltzer and Elliot (1988) estimate that approximately 14.2 per cent of the adult population have some form of disability. This means that there are approximately 6,202,000 disabled adults in Great Britain. (Disability was defined as 'A restriction or lack of ability to perform normal activities which has resulted from the impairment of a structure or function of the body or mind' (Martin *et al*. 1988: xi)). Of these, 93.2 per cent (5,780,000) live in the community and 6.8 per cent (422,000) live in institutions. Furthermore, 41.8 per cent (2,595,000) are in the 16–65 age group. 58.5 per cent (3,631,000) of disabled people are female and 41.5 per cent (2,571,000) are male.

Despite the size of the population with a disability very few are actually in work. Only 36 per cent of men and 31 per cent of women with disabilities are in employment; 52 per cent of disabled men under 30 years of age are not working.

Research also shows that legislation on disability is not adhered to by organisations and that only a minority meet the quota of employees stipulated by the Disabled Persons (Employment) Act of 1944.

Age

There is also what became known in the UK (eg Davidson 1991) as the 'demographic time bomb', referring to the falling number of younger people entering the workforce. By the year 2000 the number of 16–25-year-olds entering the labour market will have fallen by 1.5 million compared with 1987 (Employment Department 1988). This essentially means that one traditional source of new labour for organisations (ie school-leavers) is drying up.

Women

Women are making a significant and visible impact on the UK economy:

- According to Ellison (1994), between 1983 and 1990 the labour market expanded by over 2 million to reach a peak of 28.3 million people. Between 1990 and 1993 the labour force is expected to have fallen in each year. However, it is predicted to grow from 28 million in 1994 to 29.4 million in 2006. Of this increase, 1.1 million will be women and only 0.3 million men.
- In 1993 women made up 44 per cent of the labour force. By 2001 this is expected to be 45.3 per cent and by 2006 45.8 per cent.

Payne (1991) identifies some of the significant trends:

- In the 1980s the majority of new jobs created were part-time and in the service industries. The majority of these went to women.
- Women are taking less time out of work to raise families and more return to work in the interval between the births of their children.
- In 1979 24 per cent of women who had worked through their pregnancy were back at work within nine months. By 1988 this had risen to 45 per cent. However, 'women who return to work quickly are much more likely than women who take an extended career break to return to a full-time job, and they have a far better chance of maintaining their position on the occupational ladder' (Payne 1991: 9).
- Well-qualified women, when compared with an equivalent group

of men, are less likely to gain a job commensurate with their qualification: 42 per cent of men with degree-level qualifications are employed in professional-level jobs, compared with 15 per cent of women. As Payne states, 'the wastage of talent that is implied by these figures is enormous' (Payne 1991: 8).

- Self-employment and part-time work provide useful flexibility, allowing many women to combine work outside the home with domestic commitments. Self-employment among women has also grown over the years. Only 3 per cent (292,000) of women in employment were self-employed in 1979, compared with 7 per cent (805,000) in 1991.
- Of the 5.1 million part-timers in Great Britain in 1991 88 per cent were women. The number of women in part-time employment has grown by around 1 million since 1979. The number of women in full-time employment has also increased, rising from 5.6 million in 1979 to 6.3 million in 1991.
- Women in general tend to be concentrated in a narrow range of occupations and industries. Women employees are much more highly concentrated in the service sector and non-manual occupations. The clerical and service sector accounts for over half of total women's employment (52 per cent), almost three times the level for men (18 per cent). Men are more likely to occupy managerial and professional positions (36 per cent) than women (26 per cent).
- Although women have increased their participation in the labour market there is evidence to suggest that many have continued to face barriers to labour-market entry. In 1991 there were 875,000 women who said that they would have liked regular work outside the home but were at the time looking after the home or family.

Carers and eldercare

In addition to the issues presented by childcare there are those presented by eldercare ie 'the process of assisting an elderly relative or acquaintance' (Berry-Lound 1993: 7). According to Berry-Lound:

- There are approximately 6.8 million carers in the UK.
- This represents 2.9 million men and 3.9 million women.
- Approximately one adult in seven is a carer.
- One-fifth of carers are caring for more than one person.
- 23 per cent look after relations who live with them.
- Most carers are in the 45–64-year age bracket.
- Approximately 25 per cent of carers spend 20 hours a week or more on caring activities.

Summary of changes within the UK

What the above analysis shows is that the workforce in the last two decades has changed quite considerably and that further changes are to be expected in the future. There are more ethnic minorities, women, older people and people with caring responsibilities than ever before. It is likely that people from such groups will want satisfying jobs and a feeling that their employer will take an interest in their development just like everyone else. However, the route people take to achieve their goals may be quite different. As a recently published National Economic Development Organisation (1990) report stated in respect of women's careers:

> the typical British manager starts off in jobs, on training schemes or with qualifications necessary for managerial pro-motion. He (and it usually is a he) will have experience in functions seen as essential to understanding the business and will then move into a more general role. He will be continu-ously employed, work long hours, aim to reach senior man agement by 40 and be geographically mobile. He will also be a successful hurdler in the promotion race. (NEDO 1990: 21.)

The point the report goes on to make is that for some people, par-ticularly women, this will not be an attractive route to take. Conse-quently organisations will need to view career paths more flexibly than they have done previously.

Organisations can therefore no longer assume that people will continue to be motivated by the same factors, or that working patterns successful in the past will be successful in the future. In order to utilise this newly constituted workforce effectively organisations must be prepared to listen, learn and respond flexibly. These are all issues that we will return to later in this book.

Demographic changes in the USA

While the changes within the USA may be of little practical interest to many UK-based organisations it is worth delineating them because it was a growing awareness of them that first stimulated the move towards diversity. Furthermore, much of the literature on diversity stems from the USA and we will be describing the experiences of several US organisations later in this book.

The most influential report to look at demographics in the USA was produced by the Hudson Institute (Johnston and Packer 1987) and this has been the catalyst and starting-point for much of the debate on managing diversity. It showed that US-born white males are expected to comprise only 15 per cent of the new entrants into the workforce in the 1990s. In 2000 they will make up only 29 per cent of the workforce, down from 46 per cent at the start of the decade. The remaining 85 per cent of new entrants into the workforce will come from groups outside the traditional economic mainstream.

Growth rates among the different ethnic minority groups are going to be higher than among the white population. The effect of this will be felt in the next century, so that by 2020 the size of racial and ethnic groups will have doubled. By the year 2056 these groups are predicted to outnumber the white population. Black people, who now comprise 11 per cent of the labour force, will constitute 12 per cent by 2000. Hispanics will account for 23 per cent of new workforce entrants and will increase their share of the labour force to 10 per cent by 2000 (from 7 per cent in 1991). Other ethnic groups – Asians, Pacific Islanders – are predicted to grow by 70 per cent, and their share of the labour force will increase from 3 per cent in 1991 to 4 per cent in 2000 (Hammond and Kleiner 1992). This trend has been referred to as the 'browning' of America (Abassi and Hollman 1991).

There has also been a change in the pattern of immigration, with immigrants in the 1990s primarily coming from South and East Asia and Latin America; this presents language differences as well as differences in personal value systems. Because of their lower educational achievement these groups are overrepresented in slow-growing or declining occupations such as farm work, factory work and repair work. This presents a challenge for the nation as a whole precisely because these areas of work are declining (Johnston and Packer 1987).

Females are expected to enter the workforce in large numbers between 1991 and 2000. Almost two-thirds of the 15 million entrants into the workforce during this decade will be women (Johnston and Packer 1987). Women are also concentrated in the traditional female occupations and are underrepresented in several high-paying, fast-growing fields such as engineering, the medical sciences and architecture. However, they dominate in numerous other vocational and professional jobs such as insurance, computer operation, accounting and auditing, financial management, public relations and so on. Indeed these are the occupations expected to grow in the 1990s and as a consequence female dominance in these areas will continue (Abassi and Hollman 1991).

The average age of the workforce is expected to increase from 36 in 1991 to 39 by 2000. Despite that, however, it is expected that the proportion of workers aged 55 and over, who in 1991 comprised about 13 per cent of the labour force, will decline to 11 per cent by 2000 (Fullerton 1989).

The issues of demographic change have been summed up as the six 'time bombs' by Rajan (1990). Although this theory is based on European data it is very similar to the 'six policy challenges' identified by Johnston and Packer (1987). Both sets of authors agree that three of the 'time bombs' or 'policy challenges' relate specifically to the changing nature of the workforce, and in particular to:

- gender – increasing numbers of women entering the labour market
- ethnic minorities – they will be forming an increasing part of the workforce
- age – the ageing of the working population.

The changing demographic situation will have an effect on organisations and on society. Much of the work on managing diversity has stemmed from trying to identify what this impact will be and how organisations can prepare themselves for it.

The position in Europe

The demographic position is also changing across the EU according to the Commission of the European Communities (1992). For example, the EU share of global population will have fallen from 6.4 per cent in 1992 to 4.4 per cent by 2010, and by 2025 over 20 per cent of the EU population will be over 65 years of age. By 1993 there were only 1,000 net entrants to the European labour market compared with 500,000 in 1970; by the year 2000 more people will be leaving than joining the labour market. It is estimated that by the end of the decade 80 per cent of new entrants to the European labour market will be female.

Globalisation of trade

One of the other major challenges facing organisations in managing diversity is the changing nature of international trade. The free movement of labour across the EU means that organisations are employing people from the other EU nations.

There are 12 nations in the EU. The EU has nine official languages; several countries are multilingual. About 50 million of the EU population are estimated to be minority language speakers

(Mole 1990). International trade is also becoming more pluralistic. For example, in 1989 EU countries made 1,500 cross-border acquisitions worldwide, of which 754 were within the European Community (EC). The UK made by far the largest number. In addition, 206 EC companies were bought by North American companies, and 230 by companies from the rest of the world eg Sweden, Switzerland, Japan and Finland. Also, some 1,000 EU companies were involved in corporate partnerships such as joint ventures or strategic cross-share holdings (Mole 1990).

All this points to an increasing internationalisation of markets and the way organisations operate. This will mean that organisations will have to deal with managing diversity not only in their own countries but also in others, and with having people from their overseas operations working together on projects.

Key points

- The primary spur for the development of work in diversity are the demographic changes facing the USA and Western Europe in particular.
- In summary, these changes mean that there are increasing numbers of ethnic minorities and women entering the workplace, and that there is an ageing population. The basic premiss of managing diversity is that if organisations are to manage this heterogeneous workforce effectively they have to find flexible ways of operating to accommodate the needs, desires and motivations of different people to the benefit of all.
- Rajan (1990) examined the impact of workforce changes within the UK and Europe, and his conclusions (or 'time bombs' as he calls them) are similar to the 'policy challenges' drawn by Johnston and Packer (1987) from their analysis of the US data. They agree that three of the issues relate to:
  - gender ie the increasing numbers of women entering the labour market
  - ethnic minorities and the fact that they will form an increasing part of the workforce
  - the ageing of the working population.
- The changing demographic situation will have an effect on organisations and society. Much of the work on diversity has stemmed from trying to identify what this impact will be and how organisations can prepare themselves for it.

4

The Benefits Mosaic

The perceived benefits of managing diversity effectively are often quoted in the diversity literature (Jackson and Associates 1992; McEnrue 1993; Hall and Parker 1993; Cox and Blake 1991; Hammond and Kleiner 1992; Cox 1991; Mandrell and Kohler-Gray 1990; Hammond 1992). This chapter outlines the nature of these benefits and examines the evidence to support them. We will highlight those areas where:

- solid evidence exists for these benefits
- there is a need for more concrete evidence
- it may be impossible to collect conclusive evidence.

What are the perceived benefits?

In this section we present a brief overview of the array of benefits frequently quoted as resulting from managing diversity. These range from the more concrete and measurable organisational savings associated with reduced recruitment and attrition costs to those benefits that can be viewed as an anticipated logical consequence of diversity, for example increased morale.

Some writers have taken a radical, perhaps even cynical, view of the benefits: Lynch viewed managing diversity as the 'new future-orientated proportionalism' that 'helps business harness this demographic destiny by exorcising the invisible demons of institutional racism/sexism and by cleansing white male culture' (Lynch 1994: 32). Managing diversity has also been hailed as unleashing energy from employees, freeing them from the need to assimilate and play it safe (Hall and Parker 1993). It has been heralded as an enabling force for organisational change (Ross and Schneider 1992). Some writers have even linked diversity to environmental concerns (Cole

1990) and, indeed, to those of creating democratic societies (Warner 1991; Bonham-Carter 1992). Others have their feet firmly on the ground: Ross and Schneider (1992: 107) grouped the benefits into 'tangible bottomline benefits' ie the hard data and cost savings that will bring management on board.

Rosenfeld, Giacalone and Riordan (1994) noted that the language used in the diversity area 'has a rapturous quality'. The basis for their assertion was that diversity initiatives within organisations are described as not only 'celebrating' diversity, but also 'embracing', 'valuing' or indeed 'nurturing' diversity (Kennedy and Everest 1991: 50; Dominquez 1991: 16; Broadnax 1991: 10). A similar description can be given of the benefits claimed to result from managing diversity. Taken at face value, these benefits would appear to indicate that managing diversity offers a remedy for many, if not all, organisational problems!

Unfortunately, when one looks a little more closely at the research the supporting evidence for these benefits is tenuous at best and non-existent at worst. For example, McEnrue (1993) carried out an in-depth study of 15 organisations based in Los Angeles to establish the 'actual' as opposed to the 'claimed' benefits of diversity. In McEnrue's opinion the benefits cited by the organisations far outweigh those previously described in the literature. Table 4.1 outlines these 'actual' benefits.

Table 4.1
Benefits cited in McEnrue 1993

- Low labour costs, recruitment, turnover and training
  Attracting and retaining employees
- Improved understanding of customer needs
- New product development
- Improved employee relations
- Enhanced public image
- Greater creativity
- Increased capacity among managers to establish and maintain interorganisational relationships
- Lower frustration levels among supervisors, leading to reduced friction and less unwanted disciplinary action.

As with other articles in the area, it is however only in connection with the *increased access to talent* and the *reduced recruitment and associated costs* that concrete examples of benefits are provided. For example, one organisation in the study caculated the following savings as a result of managing diversity:

- reduced recruitment expenditure by 40 per cent
- reduced costs of training a large number of new recruits each year (each new recruit cost $6 thousand to train).

It was this argument, the organisational representative indicated, that caught the attention of the top management.

One paper that stands out from the rest in providing evidence for the benefits is by Cox and Blake (1991). In an article in *Academy of Management Executive* they sought to establish the link between managing diversity and organisational competitiveness. They focused their attention on six benefits, or 'arguments':

1. cost
2. resource acquisition
3. marketing
4. creativity
5. problem solving
6. organisational flexibility.

Although Cox and Blake attempted to tie down the benefits of diversity in concrete terms, persuasive examples were provided to support only the first three 'arguments'. The evidence to support the remaining three was far less substantial.

In order to make sense of the multitude of benefits cited by academics, consultants and organisations alike, we have listed the most frequently quoted and assigned them to one of three categories: proven, debatable and indirect. These are outlined in Table 4.2. The focus of our categorisation was an examination of the available evidence to support the perceived benefits.

Allport (1954: 8) stated when discussing prejudice: 'Given a thimbleful of facts we rush to make generalisations as big as a tub'.

Table 4.2
Categorisation of the perceived benefits

Proven benefits
Access to talent:
– making it easier to recruit scarce labour.
– reducing costs associated with excessive turnover and absenteeism

Flexibility:
– enhancing organisational flexibility.

Debatable benefits
Teams:
– promoting team creativity and innovation
– improving problem solving
– better decision making.

Customers:
– improving customer service
– increasing sales to members to minority culture groups.

Quality:
– improving quality.

Indirect benefits
– satisfying work environments
– improving morale and job satisfaction
– improving relations between different groups of workers
– greater productivity
– competitive edge
– better public image.

This may be the case in the diversity field: writers are quick to cite
an array of benefits, but rarely do they question or examine the
underlying evidence.

However, a few notable exceptions exist: R. R. Thomas (1992:
310) acknowledged when outlining the benefits that 'concrete data
are scarce'. V. C. Thomas (1994: 60) likened diversity to a new
drug: 'Its capabilities and benefits are highly touted but its
inescapable side-effects are hidden in the small print of a cumber-
some text – if they are known at all.'

Lack of evidence does not necessarily imply that the claims
about benefits are inaccurate or misleading; rather, by breaking

down the evidence into our three categories a clearer picture emerges
(see Table 4.3). The evidence for each of the three categories will
now be examined in turn.

Table 4.3
Available evidence

Category	Evidence
Proven benefits	– organisation savings: recruitment, attrition and training – wider pool of candidates – increased flexibility.
Debatable benefits	– based largely on ambiguous research on team effectiveness – inconclusive data on improved quality and customer service.
Indirect benefits	– difficult, if not impossible to establish.

Proven benefits

The proven benefits of diversity are those that are an unavoidable
consequence of becoming a diversity-oriented employer. Evidence
appears to weigh more favourably on the side of these direct benefits,
as they are essentially proven. Specifically, they include:

- recruiting from a wider range of talented candidates
- retaining this talent
- the associated savings from lower turnover and absenteeism.

All of these will be discussed under the heading 'Access to talent'
below. An additional direct benefit is enhanced organisational flexibility, which is discussed on pages 41–44.

Access to talent

The fundamental argument for managing diversity is the benefit derived from recruiting, retaining and promoting the best people regardless of their background, ethnicity, accent, sex, hair colour, or other individual characteristics.

As outlined in Chapter 3, the changing profile of the workforce has been a major impetus for organisations to ensure that they have access to the best of all available talent. It goes without saying that organisations which continue to rely on the traditional pool of white, able-bodied males will be ignoring valuable potential in the remaining population and will thus run the risk of losing out to competitors. Organisations that manage their diversity effectively can also improve their retention rates for different groups of people, thus reducing turnover and absenteeism costs.

McEnrue (1993) reported in her survey of organisations in the Los Angeles area that the majority of organisations gave as their primary reason for instituting managing diversity the ability to attract and retain employees in the face of labour shortages and changes in the demographic composition of the workforce. Attracting talent from the broadest range of people available will have an impact on organisations not only in terms of the quality of their workforce but also in terms of cost effectiveness, particularly with regard to training time required (Kandola 1989). Table 4.4 outlines how a large brewery reduced its training costs by developing an objective procedure for the selection of operators.

By managing diversity, organisations are not only ensuring that they recruit the best but also that the best are promoted and that the potential within each employee is harnessed. To achieve this, organisations must ensure that:

- the organisational processes (eg recruitment, selection, promotion, training, career development) are fair (ie based on objective and job-relevant criteria)
- the managers who run the processes are skilled in assessing the criteria.

The benefits of diversity thus realised are not only attracting the 'best' from a wide range of groups but also optimising the potential of these recruits at each level in the organisation.

Table 4.4

Reducing training costs in a large brewery

> The brewery was establishing a new bottling plant in an inner city area. They wanted to ensure they recruited the best applicants from the multiracial community surrounding the site. A job analysis was conducted identifying the competencies required for the job and selection procedures designed which mapped onto the competencies. Structured interview schedules were created for interviewers to use. Recruiters were trained in the use of this new process.
>
> After implementation it was found that ethnic minority candidates were as successful as others in the process. By recruiting talented people from all sections of the community it was found that training time for these new recruits was *three weeks* quicker than for people in an equivalent plant in another part of the country that did not use such a procedure.

The benefits to be had from retaining this talent are widely recognised in the literature. Ellis and Sonnenfeld (1994: 81) state that 'nurturing, promoting and ensuring the fair treatment of women and minorities goes as far to advance the firm's competitive edge as it does to advance the careers of these employees'. And the corporate vice-president of Digital, a pioneer of diversity training, has said: 'When white males understand that 40% of their sales force is responsible for about a billion and a half dollars in orders, it becomes an obvious bottom-line goal to keep them happy, motivated and productive' (Thomas 1991: 115).

Failure to retain and develop valuable talent means a failure to secure any reasonable return on investment. Data available from both the UK and the USA suggests that many organisations are losing out by failing to retain women and ethnic minorities (see Table 4.5).

Table 4.5
Examples of poor retention

- Corning Glass reported that during the period 1980–7 turnover amongst black people was 2.5 times higher than among white, and for women it was double that of men. It was data such as this that jolted them into managing their diversity. (Cox and Blake 1991)
- Surveys carried out by Trost (1990) indicated higher turnover rates for women at all ages. The primary reason for leaving given by these women was the lack of opportunity for career progression.
- A retail bank in the UK estimated that they lost £3 million each year because of failure to retain part of their female workforce after maternity leave.
- Schwartz (1992) has stated that in management positions the female-to-male turnover ratio is 2:1.
- A recent survey conducted by the Institute of Management (1994) showed that the percentage of women managers and directors in the UK is on the decline, falling from 10.2 per cent in 1993 to 9.5 per cent in 1994. Roger Young, the director general of the Institute, suggests that women may be leaving because organisations are not meeting their needs.

The research indicates that organisations have allowed women (and ethnic minorities) to walk straight out the back door, and many studies suggest this may be due to a perceived lack of career progression, which itself may be the result of stereotypical judgements about what constitutes a suitable career path for a woman. Powell (1990: 72) believes that for organisations to unleash the potential of all their employees they will need to shatter the previously held notion that women have 'a monopoly on human resource skills'; this belief, he asserts, has lead to the pigeon-holing of women into managerial roles that require interpersonal skills (eg personnel or customer relations) and has ultimately kept women out of the more powerful line functions and the boardroom.

More generally, research has also indicated it is not just ethnic minorities and women that organisations may risk losing if they do not manage their diversity effectively. Syrett and Lammiman (1994) refer to recent research carried out by the London Human Resource Group indicating that there was an increase in turnover to almost

50 per cent of City-based staff between 1992 and 1993. The research concludes that staff lack faith in their organisations' efforts at empowerment and development, and that employees were moving to organisations that were perceived as providing better opportunities.

However, evidence exists of the benefits for organisations which ensure they retain *all* their staff by providing an environment in which their potential is realised. Hall and Parker (1993) cite the experiences of Corning Inc. as an example of the cost benefits to be achieved from effectively managing diversity (see Table 4.6). Ortho Pharmaceuticals have also been cited by Cox and Blake (1991) as saving $500,000, mainly from lower turnover of women and ethnic minorities.

Table 4.6

Evidence of retention from Corning Inc.

- Corning Inc. were incurring an annual cost of $3.5–$4 million from losing women professionals at twice the rate of white males.
- The problem was tackled by implementing a corporate initiative to ensure that each individual had the opportunity to 'participate fully, to grow professionally, and to develop his or her highest potential'.
- The results thus far indicate an increase in the recruitment, retention and advancement of women and African-Americans.

A 1988 report by the Industrial Relations Services reported that one private-sector employer estimated their annual loss of 1,000 women managers cost them £17 million every year, whereas a survey of 100 organisations by the Industrial Relations Services in 1990 found that a policy of flexible working was the most effective measure for recruiting and retaining women. And in a report on flexibility at senior and managerial levels carried out by New Ways to Work (1993) 81 per cent of the 106 respondents cited retention as the main advantage from introducing flexible work arrangements.

Flexibility of the organisation

One way the diversity-oriented organisation has ensured the retention of employees is through enhanced flexibility. As the workforce becomes increasingly diverse there has been greater pressure on organisations to respond by being more flexible in all their processes, systems and procedures, and not only in their working hours. In fact, a report by Towers Perrin/CBI (1992) on employee benefits (company car, pension, life assurance etc) reported that organisations are now offering flexible employee benefits in order to respond to the changing needs of their workforce.

Watson (1994) has recently updated the figures on the size of the flexible workforce in the UK; the 1993 Labour Force Survey data formed the basis of his analysis. Watson established that 38 per cent of all people in employment are in the flexible workforce ie an increase of 1.25 million individuals since 1986. The proportion of men in the flexible workforce has risen substantially from 18 per cent in 1981 to 27 per cent in 1993. While the proportion of women has stayed fairly constant (about 50 per cent) there are differences in the type of flexible working that men and women are carrying out. Eighty-five per cent of part-timers are women whereas three-quarters of the self-employed are men.

The importance of organisational flexibility has been recognised for some time. Herriot (1989) stated it was imperative that the terms and conditions of employment offered by organisations were responsive to individual needs. If they were not, he concluded, organisations ran the risk of failing to meet the human resources demands of the 1990s. Ross and Schneider (1992: 105) put it succinctly: 'if there is not sufficient flexibility within an organisation, the best will go elsewhere'.

The introduction of flexible working practices by organisations has provided solid evidence of the benefits to be gained from managing diversity, especially in terms of reduced turnover and absenteeism. The majority of cases cited to support this contention refer to the improved retention rates of women that have been achieved by offering flexibility in work hours and practices. Cox and Blake (1991) also provide evidence of the benefits to be achieved from what they call 'organisational accommodations' to diversity (ie flexibility). They cite the following studies:

- absenteeism reduced by the provision of child daycare (Young-blood and Chambers-Cook 1984).
- both short- and long-term absenteeism down significantly as a result of flexitime (Kim and Campagna 1981).

While the above examples are from the USA evidence is also available in the UK.

- Hammond and Holton (1991) give the example of a major UK bank that found investing in childcare led to higher retention rates for staff and that this was cheaper than continually recruiting and training new staff.
- Petrofina (UK) Ltd introduced flexible work patterns for drivers, depot workers and plant operators, and found that productivity rose by 20 per cent (Curson 1988).
- Sainsbury's report that the numbers of employees returning to work after maternity leave increased from 42 per cent in 1989/90 to 74 per cent in 1991/2 as a result of flexible working options. Sainsbury's invest millions of pounds each year in training and there were obvious financial advantages in keeping this trained workforce (Donaldson 1993).
- In 1989 Boots found that only 4 per cent of their shop assistants returned after maternity leave. By introducing a range of flexible working options the proportion had risen to 49 per cent in 1993 (New Ways to Work 1993).
- The National Westminster Bank states that flexible working has succeeded on a variety of fronts, including opening for longer hours, matching people on duty with the busier periods and in meeting staff needs in balancing work and personal life (Don-aldson 1993).

Adopting a strategic approach to flexibility.   While the benefits of flexibility have been firmly established Hall and Parker (1993) claim that more can be achieved for both employers and employees by adopting a more strategic approach to organisational flexibility. These authors suggest a radical departure from what is traditionally conceived as flexibility. In their opinion organisations should move towards being 'employee-friendly' rather than just 'family-friendly'. They argue that relating flexibility just to work/family issues as opposed to work/life issues not only alienates those who do not have families but may also communicate to employees that the only legitimate outside interest they can have is a family. However, in outlining the changes involved in achieving a more strategic approach they recognise that an initial narrow focus (eg childcare) can eventually evolve into enhanced flexibility of working practices for all employees.

The benefits that they claim can be achieved by a broader strategic approach include higher levels of psychological engagement, increased work performance and ultimately 'a more responsive, adaptable environment' (Hall and Parker 1993: 16). Benefits in terms of cost savings are also claimed as a direct result of 'more effective recruitment, retention, and attendance, and an improved corporate image' (Hall and Parker 1993: 15). While they do not give a profile of their vision of a truly flexible organisation, their proposal appears responsive to the needs of all employees and not just specific groups. This fits in very closely with our definition of managing diversity.

Hall and Parker provide a welcome reminder to organisations that a strategic approach is critical and that 'flexibility' with a narrow focus is insufficient. However, recent research in the UK reveals that organisations do not view flexibility in a strategic fashion. Research by McGregor and Sproull (1992) indicates that it is viewed as a solution to a specific problem. The same conclusion was reached by Brewster and Hegewisch (1993) in their survey of HR practices across Europe. They stated that: 'At the company level, our data shows that the growth of flexibility has little correlation with strategic HR policies: it appears to be, in general, an ad hoc response to external pressures. Flexible working practices clearly are seen by many organisations across Europe as a more efficent way of working, but to be successful they need careful management and investment in administration and training' (Brewster and Hegewisch 1993: 38). However, as Hall and Parker (1993) point out, this narrow approach could be the first stage in achieving true organisational flexibility. Indeed, as more and more organisations begin to recognise the benefits that can be achieved it is likely their vision of the flexible organisation may not be too far from realisation.

Debatable benefits

The debatable benefits are those thought to result from having a mix of people with a wide range of styles, backgrounds, personalities etc in the workforce. The majority of these benefits are indicated in team research that essentially shows heterogeneous or diverse teams outperform homogeneous teams. This research will be examined more closely on pages 46–50. First we outline two debatable benefits that do not rely on team research: increased quality and improved customer service.

Increased quality

Managing diversity is thought to feed into successful Total Quality Management (TQM), that is, achieving quality in terms of product, customer service, and the workforce. The argument is based on the rationale that TQM not only requires an organisation's systems and regulations be reviewed and improved but that this approach be supported and implemented by all its employees. By managing diversity an organisation not only employs the best but also achieves the best from full utilisation of its workforce, which increases the chances of achieving its quality objectives. In essence it is the workforce that makes quality happen.

Jackson (1992) goes so far as to state that one cannot achieve TQM without managing diversity. Her rationale is that if organisations fail to manage diversity they will be punishing their 'internal customers' via lack of support, lack of opportunity for career progression, and discrimination, and that this in turn will reduce the quality of service they provide to 'external customers'. While the argument has much to commend it in terms of its logic and rationale there is unfortunately little or no data to support it.

Improved customer service

Managing diversity is thought by some to enable an organisation to get closer to its customers and thus improve its customer service. This contention is based on two premisses: the move to a service economy and an increased understanding of existing and potential markets.

In the current UK economy, where the shift has been away from manufacturing towards the service industry (Ross and Schneider 1992), effective communications between people are crucial to business success. It is not only important to have effective external communications, for example between employees and customers, but also good internal communications between employees themselves. The management of diversity is therefore thought to be paramount, as it is the skills and abilities of each individual employee that will make the difference.

Bell (1973) is quoted by Jackson and Alvarez (1992) as describing the service industry as a 'game between two people'. The authors add: 'to win this game, they [organisations] need employees that can read their customers and interact with them in a nearly flawless manner' (Jackson and Alvarez 1992: 14). They argue that the diversity-oriented organisation will have such employees and will ultimately reap the associated benefits.

One of the main driving forces behind managing diversity – population changes – also highlights changes in the customer base. A potent example of the potential impact of increasing customer diversity is that of London Weekend Television. An estimate of the makeup of their audience indicated that ethnic minorities would constitute 25 per cent by the year 2000. This was in sharp contrast to the 5 per cent ethnic minority mix within their existing workforce. As Ross and Schneider (1992) point out, this highlights a real risk for the organisation in terms of losing contact with their customers' needs.

A report published by the Ethnic Minority Business Development Initiative in 1991 also indicated that many UK financial institutions were losing out to competitors because they failed to meet the needs of the black community. The report highlighted the need for banks to understand the needs of all customers if they are to obtain business from ethnic minority communities.

Organisations that understand their markets obviously have a competitive advantage over those who do not. It is claimed that having an organisation in which the workforce mirrors the market-place is an asset in anticipating and servicing customer needs and demands. Creating a more accurate microcosm within organisations of the society in which they seek to operate will, it is predicted, not only enhance communication with customers, but also limit the potential for alienating them through inaccurate understanding or stereotyping of their needs.

The ability of an organisation to provide products and services to all potential markets is a bottom-line concern. While the evidence is slight, it does suggest that the diversity-oriented organisation should be more responsive to the diverse needs of its customer base. However, no conclusive data is yet available.

Improved team effectiveness

Advocates of managing diversity believe that it will lead to improved creativity, innovation, problem solving and decision making within organisations (Cox and Blake 1991; Thomas 1991; Ross and Schneider 1992; Hammond 1992). The bulk of the evidence for this claim hinges on the findings of academic research into team effectiveness. As stated previously, however, though writers are quick to cite the research, few have examined it closely. It is therefore appropriate that we do so here.

The findings of the research cited have been synthesised and listed in Table 4.7. In synthesising the research we focused on these factors:

- how heterogeneity was defined
- which type of team (ie heterogeneous or homogeneous) produced the better outcome
- how performance was improved.

Table 4.7

A summary of research into team effectiveness

How is heterogeneity defined?	Better outcome			In what way was performance improved?
	By heterogeneous team	By homogeneous team	No difference	
Belbin (1981): personality types and roles	✓	✓✓		More successful team but homogeneous teams were also successful when they consisted of stable extroverts who enjoy working in teams and whose roles may be undifferentiated, and when they consisted of many talented people.
Kanter (1983): roles – specialists and generalists	✓			Increased innovation.
Saavedra (1990): working style and age			✓	Better at solving problems and overcoming obstacles.
Nemeth (1986): attitude ie not subscribing to the strategy advocated by the majority	✓			More creative.
Hoffman and Maier (1961): sex and personality	✓			Better quality solutions to assigned problems.
Watson et al. (1993): nationality and ethnic background Nemeth (1986): attitude		✓		Few short-term problems: establishing relationships and appropriate processes. Better task performance among **newly** formed groups.
Adler (1986): culture			✓	Productivity: some heterogeneous teams were more productive, some were less.

Table 4.7 highlights the inconclusiveness of the data. Four of the studies indicated that the heterogeneous team outperformed the homogeneous team, three studies indicated the reverse and two found no difference between teams. Moreover, while some writers defined heterogeneity in terms of sex and personality others defined it in terms of attitude or organisational role.

Are we any the wiser? Can we really assert, as other diversity writers have, that diversity *will* automatically result in increased team creativity, problem solving etc? A number of issues regarding this research need to be highlighted before any conclusions can be reached. These include:

- defining what we mean by heterogeneity
- identifying the conditions under which heterogeneity is advantageous.

Defining heterogeneity. Within the team-research literature itself there seems to be little overlap in how the various studies define heterogeneity. As highlighted above, this heterogeneity can be seen in terms of attitude, work role or personality as well as sex and ethnicity. However, writers on diversity cite this research as evidence for the benefits of having mixed teams of women and men from different ethnic backgrounds.

There appears to be some inconsistency here. The various research studies provide evidence only for the heterogeneous factors they sought to investigate. Moreover, the research was carried out (in the main) on white male groups: the quintessence of homogeneity in the eyes of advocates of diversity. Based on this analysis, therefore, the team research seems fully to support the following statement:

> An all-white male team composed of people of different thinking styles and personalities can perform more effectively than a mixed team of men and women of different ethnic origins who basically share the same personality traits and thinking styles.

Therefore the assertion that having a mix of sexes and ethnic groups on a team will automatically result in improved team effectiveness does *not* appear to be supported by the available evidence. The different sexes and ethnic groupings may indeed bring different and valuable perspectives to a team situation. Ultimately, however, it is only to the individual that we should attribute these benefits.

Identifying the conditions under which heterogeneity is advantageous. A second issue emerging from the research is the dilemma of maintaining cohesiveness while at the same time avoiding 'group think' (Janis 1972). In researching the effectiveness of heterogeneous and homogeneous teams a number of writers have highlighted the problem of ensuring that heterogeneity does not impede progress (Bettenhausen 1991; Shepard 1964). Whilst an overemphasis on group cohesion may be one of the challenges avoided by having heterogeneous teams, how to achieve consensus is another challenge that has been highlighted.

Bettenhausen (1991: 356), in his detailed review of group research, recognised that the advantages of heterogeneity may be outweighed by the problem of how to achieve consensus: 'diversity hinders group and organisational performance, especially in times of crisis or rapid change.' Indeed, given that for many people the focus for the benefits has been exclusively on differences, it is ironic to find that Shepard (1964) stresses the importance of similarity in helping to develop group cohesion. This cohesion is in turn found to be related to the success of a group.

Research would also seem to indicate that diverse teams have greater short-term problems, particularly with establishing relationships and appropriate processes, than more homogeneous groups (eg Watson, Kumar and Michaelson 1993; Hoffman and Maier 1961; Nemeth 1986). Adler (1986) found that this problem was exaggerated when differences of nationality and culture are coupled to those of personality and style of working. It appears then that the greater the diversity the more time is needed to establish the ground rules and the more difficult it is to reach consensus.

It is not our assertion that these difficulties are insurmountable but rather that they should be recognised by writers in the diversity field and that action should be taken to overcome them. As Bettenhausen

(1991: 356) concludes: 'because increased pluralism is an unavoidable fact of organisational life, it is not very helpful to merely acknowledge that "process losses" may outweigh the benefits of heterogeneity. Rather, concerted effort is needed to explore how diverse perspectives can be shared more effectively.' Shepard (1964: 118) summed up the issue: 'Variety is the spice of life in a group, so long as there is a basic core of similarity.'

It does not appear possible to assert on the basis of the research findings that diversity will in itself lead to improved team performance. The most we feel able to say is: 'it depends.' The data is far from conclusive. As Hill (1982) concluded, the effectiveness of a team depends on a wide range of factors, not just whether its membership is heterogeneous in sex and ethnicity. This point has been emphasised by others, for example Buller (1986). Many factors in addition to sex and ethnicity have been identified as having an impact on team effectiveness:

- the nature of the task
- the ability of team members
- the personality traits of team members
- the length of time the group stays together
- the urgency of the task
- the organisational roles of the team members
- the team leader.

Rather than boldly asserting that diversity will automatically increase team effectiveness, energy needs to be channelled into providing a solid research base from which the benefits can be clearly outlined.

Indirect benefits

The indirect benefits are those believed to result when the direct and debatable benefits have been achieved. They are thought to be a logical consequence of having an organisation in which the best possible candidates are selected, developed and retained, and in which quality of service and output are maximised. The indirect benefits are based on a rational argument that can be presented as a flow chart (see Figure 4.1).

Figure 4.1
Links between the diversity benefits

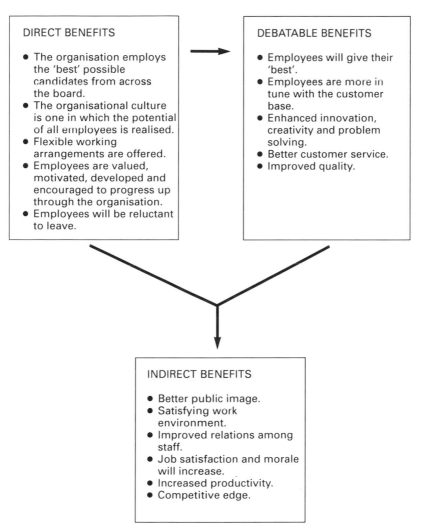

DIRECT BENEFITS

- The organisation employs the 'best' possible candidates from across the board.
- The organisational culture is one in which the potential of all employees is realised.
- Flexible working arrangements are offered.
- Employees are valued, motivated, developed and encouraged to progress up through the organisation.
- Employees will be reluctant to leave.

DEBATABLE BENEFITS

- Employees will give their 'best'.
- Employees are more in tune with the customer base.
- Enhanced innovation, creativity and problem solving.
- Better customer service.
- Improved quality.

INDIRECT BENEFITS

- Better public image.
- Satisfying work environment.
- Improved relations among staff.
- Job satisfaction and morale will increase.
- Increased productivity.
- Competitive edge.

As can be deduced from Figure 4.1 it is argued that increased morale, job satisfaction, employee harmony, and ultimately productivity and competitiveness are natural consequences of providing an environment in which *all* employees are given the opportunity to develop and progress through the organisation.

Many of the indirect benefits could easily be those expected of any organisational change initiative. And, as is well documented, it is very difficult with such initiatives to establish solid evidence linking the benefits directly to the change that was implemented. Because of this problem of causality the indirect benefits are by their very nature tenuous and the links may never be firmly established.

Conclusion

Evidence cited for the debatable and indirect benefits is at best very sketchy and at worst non-existent. As it stands this evidence is unlikely to persuade senior management to embark on a managing diversity programme. Unsubstantiated claims for the benefits of diversity have two negative effects: first, they divert attention from the areas of real, proven and direct benefits (ie access to talent and organisational flexibility). Whenever an organisation embarks on a diversity programme these are the very minimum expectations it should have. Second, if organisations expect to obtain the other benefits – those we have called debatable and indirect – they may well end up being disappointed. The increased expectations at the start will merely fuel discontent, disillusion and dissatisfaction later. By not overhyping the benefits and by recognising the areas where more information is needed and more attention required we will create a firm basis on which to build, rather than construct a house on a foundation of sand.

Key points

- A host of benefits have been claimed to result from managing diversity.
- Taken at face value they appear to offer a panacea for organisational problems.
- The benefits can be broken down into three categories:
  - proven
  - debatable
  - indirect.
- It is necessary to look beneath the stated benefits at the supporting evidence.
- The most solid evidence available supports the proven benefits.
- Evidence supporting the debatable benefits is largely based on ambiguous data from team research. Inconclusive evidence is available to support benefits relating to increased quality and improved customer service.
- Conclusive evidence for the indirect benefits may be impossible to collect.
- Rather than overstating and perhaps diluting the benefits more attention and energy need to be channelled into establishing solid evidence. This evidence will not only serve to fill gaps in our current knowledge, but will also help fuel the management of diversity in organisations.

5

Diversity Initiatives

Introduction

In order to discover what diversity initiatives organisations are implementing, and also how successful these initiatives have been, we undertook a managing diversity survey of organisations throughout the UK. The results of the survey will be presented under the following headings:

- survey development
- the most and least frequently implemented initiatives
- initiatives perceived to be the most and the least successful
- initiatives the least and the most likely to be assessed
- reasons for taking action
- monitoring
- priority areas for future action.

Survey development

There were several stages in the design of the survey questionnaire. First a literature review was undertaken of sex, ethnicity, age, religion and disability in order to identify the key actions that organisations should be taking in managing a diverse workforce. Interviews were also carried out with a selection of organisations and institutions who are authoritative in the field.

The opinions and ideas from both the interviews and the literature review were consolidated into the 40 initiatives that formed the basis of our managing diversity questionnaire. These initiatives were those considered important in developing a diversity-oriented organisation. Examples of the initiatives included in the questionnaire are:

- the introduction of an explicit policy on harassment
- the provision of fair selection training to recruiters
- the provision of assistance with childcare.

The questionnaire also included a section on background details of the respondents. Details requested included the size and sector of the organisation, the reasons for taking action in each specific area, how initiatives were monitored and evaluated, and their priorities for the future.

The questionnaire was then piloted with 12 managers active in the diversity/equal opportunities area. (These were either equal opportunities officers or people working in personnel with equal opportunities responsibilities, and were chosen because of their expertise in equality and diversity.) They completed the questionnaire and returned it to us with feedback on how it could be improved. Their comments were incorporated in the development of the final version of the questionnaire.

Approximately 2,000 organisations were sent the questionnaire, of whom 285 replied. A good spread was obtained of small, medium-sized and large enterprises (see Figure 5.1). A mix of organisational sectors was also achieved, with approximately 60 per cent from the private sector and 40 per cent from the public sector. A breakdown of respondents by organisational sector and their employee mix is outlined in the Appendix.

Figure 5.1
Size of respondent organisations: number of employees

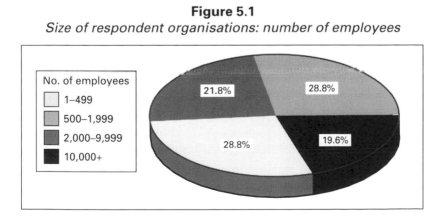

The most and least frequently implemented initiatives

The 10 most frequently implemented initiatives (see Table 5.1)

While the questionnaire was clearly framed as a managing diversity survey, the wording of some of the initiatives included reference to 'equal opportunities'. The rationale for this was that as diversity is a relatively new area within the UK and an evolutionary step beyond equal opportunities we expected organisations to have a mix of both approaches. Moreover, specific initiatives in the questionnaire could apply equally under a diversity or equality policy.

Table 5.1

The 10 most frequently implemented initiatives

		% implemented	n (=285)
1.	Having a policy on equal opportunities.	94	268
2.	Having equal opportunities monitoring in place.	76	218
3.	Having a strategy on equal opportunities.	74	212
4.	Giving fair selection training to recruiters.	74	212
5.	Physically changing the work environment eg with ramps, wide doors.	69	197
6.	Eliminating age criteria from selection decisions.	68	193
7.	Introducing an explicit policy on harassment.	67	191
8.	Introducing other flexible arrangements eg homeworking, annual hours, flexitime, term-time working.	66	189
9.	Allowing time off for caring for dependents beyond that required by law eg extended maternity/paternity leave.	64	183
10.	Having ongoing contact with local/national specialist groups eg Commission for Racial Equality, disability groups etc.	64	183

The most frequently implemented initiative was a policy on equal opportunities (94 per cent). This raises an intriguing question relating to the other 6 per cent who are taking actions: is it possible to be operating as an equal opportunities employer without having an equal opportunities policy? Having a policy could be taken as a statement of intent and a possible indication of the importance the organisation places on these issues. Not having a policy, however, does not necessarily mean that the organisation is not operating in a fair, objective and equal way towards all its employees in the conduct of its business. It must be remembered that equal opportunities does not exist as an entity by itself. It depends on the behaviour of individuals, the processes that an organisation has in place and the general treatment of people at work. While it is surely true that having an equal opportunities policy does not mean you are a genuine equal opportunities employer, the converse may well be true too: not having an equal opportunities policy does not necessarily mean that you are not an equal opportunities employer.

Some of the other most commonly implemented initiatives relate to the behaviour of people at work, for example, the way that recruiters should behave, having a policy on harassment, and ensuring that age criteria are not included in selection decisions. These actions are sending clear signals to people within organisations about how they should conduct themselves and what information they should be taking into account when making decisions.

A central theme of some of the other actions is flexibility, for example allowing time off beyond that required by law for staff to care for dependents.

The 10 least frequently implemented initiatives
(see Table 5.2)

A surprising number of the 10 least frequently implemented initiatives relate to communication, information and networking, for example helping employees on career breaks to establish networks; setting up specific employee support groups; providing skills updating for those who have been out of the workforce for some

time; surveying or canvassing opinion from the staff and public;
and requesting information from people on special needs they may
have for interviews.

Table 5.2

The 10 least frequently implemented initiatives

		% implemented	n (=285)
1.	Assisting employees on career breaks to establish networks	15	42
2.	Setting up specific employee support groups.	23	65
3.	Employing helpers/signers for those who need them.	24	68
4.	Undertaking access training to facilitate success of underrepresented groups in selection.	24	68
5.	Providing skills updating for those who have been out of the workforce for some time.	25	71
6.	Assessing managers on equal opportunities as part of their appraisal.	26	75
7.	Setting targets for the composition of the workforce.	31	89
8.	Automatically requesting information on special needs for interviews, meetings etc – eg interpreters, access.	33	95
9.	Providing assistance with childcare.	34	97
10.	Surveying/canvassing opinion from staff/public on equal opportunities.	36	103

It may be concluded that whereas organisations appeared to be
collecting statistical monitoring data quite frequently (see Table
5.1), they are not seeking out information from staff, potential
employees and the public on what they could do further. As will be
outlined in Chapter 6, the communication element of managing
diversity is crucial, not only in enabling a two-way flow of information with the workforce but also in spreading ownership.

It is perhaps not surprising to find amongst the list of least frequently taken actions those relating to more contentious, indeed controversial, issues such as target setting and positive action. However, a rather surprising discovery is that a very small proportion of organisations are providing assistance with childcare.

Initiatives perceived to be the most and the least successful

The 10 most successful initiatives (see Table 5.3)

The most successful initiatives were defined as those which organisations had said were either very successful (ie had surpassed the objectives set) or were successful (ie the objectives were achieved). In general, it is possible to put the actions in Table 5.3 into four categories:

- universal benefit
- flexibility of working
- actions relating to disability
- training.

Universal benefit.   It is clear that actions relating to equalising treatment between staff or, looked at another way, actions of universal benefit, are those seen as successful. For example:

- introducing equal rights and benefits for part-time workers compared with full-time workers
- providing benefits for partners who are the same sex, as well as for different-sex partners
- eliminating age criteria from selection procedures.

These actions ensure that all staff, whatever their status at work, their age or sexual orientation will be treated equally and that any barriers to equal treatment will be eliminated.

Table 5.3

The 10 most successful initiatives

		% rated as successful	n*
1.	Introducing equal rights and benefits for part-time workers (compared with full-time workers).	67	104
2.	Allowing flexibility in uniform/dress requirements.	66	81
3.	Allowing time off for caring for dependents beyond that required by law eg extended maternity/paternity leave.	64	103
4.	Benefits provided for employees' partners are equally available to same-sex and different-sex partners.	63	57
5.	Buying specialised equipment eg braille keyboards.	62	68
6.	Employing helpers/signers for those who need them.	61	38
7.	Training trainers in equal opportunities.	61	71
8.	Eliminating age criteria from selection decisions.	57	95
9.	Providing assistance with childcare.	55	52
10.	Allowing staff to take career breaks.	54	63
	Giving fair selection training to recruiters.	54	105
* The n varies across initiatives depending on the number of organisations that have implemented each initiative.			

Flexibility of working. Issues to do with flexibility emerge a number of times, for example:

- allowing flexibility in uniform and dress requirements
- allowing flexibility in caring for dependents.

Other actions included assistance with childcare and career breaks.

It is interesting, and, it must be said, somewhat reassuring that actions relating to flexibility emerged as amongst the most successful. It is our view that *flexibility is one of the central and most critical elements of managing diversity.* In other words, an organisation that can respond flexibly to the needs of its employees will have a greater probability of managing diversity successfully.

Once again, these initiatives can be applied universally. While it may well benefit women more to have assistance with childcare there are men who will respond favourably to this as well; caring for dependents may well benefit some groups more than others but it is something that is universally available should the need arise. It is not wholly or specifically targeted at one group based on its ethnicity or gender; instead it is based on providing assistance to staff according to their individual needs, requirements and possibly even preferences.

Actions relating to disability. These are very specific initiatives taken for individuals with disabilities, such as employing helpers and signers or buying specialised equipment. Such actions have been successful, which is understandable, in that *the needs of one individual are being met very directly.* The likelihood of such a specific individual action being successful must be relatively high.

Training. Finally, training (particularly that given to recruiters and trainers) is something that was also seen as successful. Training is obviously important in an organisation, and if equal opportunities and diversity issues can be incorporated into other forms of training by the trainers then the messages must surely be reinforced within the organisation. Similarly the issue of fair selection training for recruiters should enable them to carry out selection with greater objectivity and fairness.

It is also interesting to note that of the 10 most successful initiatives, only three appear in the 10 most frequently taken initiatives. These are:

- allowing time off for caring for dependents beyond that required by law
- eliminating age criteria from selection decisions
- giving fair selection training to recruiters.

Indeed two of the actions in the most successful initiatives appear in the least frequently taken initiatives. These are:

- employing helpers and signers for those who need them
- allowing staff to take career breaks.

This is potentially a very significant finding as there appears to be scope for organisations to look more closely at initiatives which seem to be successful and perhaps to try to carry out more of them. These successful, yet less frequent, initiatives mainly relate to flexibility eg allowing staff to take career breaks, allowing flexibility in dress and allowing time off for caring for dependants.

The 10 least successful initiatives (see Table 5.4)

These were initiatives rated as either not successful (ie objectives not met) or partially successful (ie some objectives met). It is interesting to note that a high proportion of these initiatives could be seen as focused on particular groups. For example:

- setting targets for the composition of the workforce
- using positive action in recruitment
- contributing to recruitment fairs for underrepresented groups
- undertaking access training for underrepresented groups
- providing work experience for underrepresented groups.

This is in contrast to the most successful initiatives, which could be seen as being of universal benefit, applicable to all individuals within the organisation. Approximately half of the least successful initiatives could be seen as being focused on specific groups within the organisation to the exclusion of others. Indeed providing positive action training to employees was just outside the 10 least successful initiatives. This could well generate feelings of unfairness amongst those excluded.

The other interesting issue to emerge from the list of least successful initiatives is the failure to have equal opportunities strategies and to include these strategics in business plans. This could well be an indication that the importance of equal opportunities and diversity

Table 5.4

The 10 least successful initiatives

	% rated as unsuccessful	n*
1. Setting targets for the composition of the workforce.	60	47
2. Using positive action in recruitment advertising.	55	77
3. Having a strategy on equal opportunities.	54	98
4. Contributing to recruitment/careers fairs for underrepresented groups.	53	57
5. Undertaking access training to facilitate the success of underrepresented groups in selection.	53	34
6. Including equal opportunities as part of business plans.	47	58
7. Appointing a co-ordinator for various activities.	47	54
8. Having ongoing contact with local/national specialist groups eg Commission for Racial Equality, disability groups etc.	47	78
9. Using schemes to give underrepresented groups work experience.	46	71
10. Providing skills updating for those who have been out of the workforce for some time.	45	28
* The n varies across initiatives depending on the number of organisations that have implemented each initiative.		

as central business issues has not yet been grasped or developed sufficiently by organisations to make them totally effective.

In our experience organisational strategies on such issues have not related the objectives of the equal opportunities strategy to the broader organisational goals. As a consequence the strategy will naturally be seen as peripheral to the main business of the organisation. When working with organisations we regularly ask them to carry out a self-evaluation on their performance in developing strategies in equal opportunities or, increasingly, in diversity. (This self-evaluation is based on the model described in Chapter 6.) We regularly find that organisations score themselves highest on taking initiatives but give themselves low scores on:

- setting objectives that are clear and tie in with the overall objectives of the business
- communicating with staff on what has been happening
- evaluating the results of the actions taken.

Taken together, this appears to indicate that organisations:

- take actions with little or no idea about how they meet or contribute to the overall business objectives
- do little or no evaluation, having taken the actions, of how successful they have been.

In short, too many organisations have what can best be described as
initiative-led strategies; in other words, they have taken action for
the sake of taking action.

Initiatives least likely and most likely to be assessed

Initiatives least likely to be assessed

It is interesting to examine the initiatives that organisations have
not assessed at all. At one extreme (Table 5.5) approximately one-
third of organisations have not assessed the effectiveness of their
harassment policies. About the same proportion have not made any
assessment of the effectiveness of including equal opportunities as
part of managers' appraisals. More than a quarter have not assessed
the effectiveness of having employee support groups or including
equal opportunities as part of business plans.

Approximately a fifth of organisations have not made any assessment of the awareness training they are giving to staff. Evaluation is
a vital stage in any change initiative yet it appears that organisations
are taking a piecemeal approach to their managing diversity/equal
opportunities initiatives. This is a very dangerous approach and

Table 5.5

Initiatives least likely to be assessed

		% no assess-ment made	n*
1.	Having an explicit policy on harassment.	32	52
2.	Assessing managers on equal opportunities as part of their appraisal.	30	18
3.	Setting up specific employee support groups.	26	14
4.	Including equal opportunities as part of business plans.	26	32
5.	Giving guaranteed interviews for all members of specific groups who meet shortlisting criteria eg people with disabilities.	23	29
6.	Helping employees on career breaks to establish networks.	23	8
7.	Automatically requesting information on special needs for interviews, meetings etc – eg interpreters, access.	22	20
8.	Having a policy on equal opportunities.	19	48
9.	Introducing awareness training for staff.	19	22
10.	Benefits provided for employees' partners are equally available to same-sex and different-sex partners.	19	23

* The n varies across initiatives depending on the number of organisations that have implemented each initiative.

may result in them doing the right things wrong or the wrong things right or even the wrong things wrong. They just won't be in a position to tell.

Initiatives most likely to be assessed

Issues to do with flexible working and positive action-type initiatives are those most likely to be assessed (Table 5.6). This may be one reason why there is so much more data available on the benefits of flexible working than on other areas connected with managing diversity.

Positive action training, as it is such a contentious issue, probably needs more justification before it can be carried out and as a consequence requires much more evidence in terms of evaluation.

Table 5.6
Initiatives most likely to be assessed

		% no assessment made	n*
1.	Physically changing the work environment eg ramps, wide doors	8	14
2.	Introducing job sharing/part-time work.	9	14
3.	Appointing a co-ordinator for various activities.	10	12
4.	Providing assistance with childcare.	10	9
5.	Undertaking positive-action training.	11	12
6.	Employing helpers/signers for those who need them.	11	11
7.	Giving fair selection training to recruiters.	11	21
8.	Having equal opportunities monitoring in place.	12	24
9.	Using schemes to give underrepresented groups work experience.	12	18
10.	Training trainers in equal opportunities.	12	14
11.	Introducing equal rights and benefits for part-time workers (compared with full-time workers).	12	18
12.	Introducing flexibility in training to meet the needs of different groups eg style, time, medium, venue.	12	12

* The n varies across initiatives depending on the number of organisations that have implemented each initiative.

Reasons for taking action

From the data three reasons stand out as to why organisations have taken action (see Table 5.7). Probably most encouraging is the fact that nearly 40 per cent of organisations see it as representing *good business sense*. Obviously these organisations see that there is some organisational benefit to be gained in implementing such initiatives. This figure of approximately 40 per cent would be much higher if developing the potential of individuals, responding to and reflecting community and consumer needs, improving service to customers,

Table 5.7
Reasons for taking action

		%	n (= 277)
1.	Good business sense.	40	110
2.	Legislation.	34	93
3.	Senior management commitment.	27	74
4.	Good practice.	11	31
5.	Fair and caring treatment of staff/corporate values/culture.	8	21
6.	Responding to/reflecting community and consumer needs.	8	21
7.	Organisational image.	7	19
8.	Developing potential of individuals.	6	16
9.	Pressure from the centre/other parts of the organisation.	6	16
10.	Pressure from members.	5	15
11.	Recruitment and retention.	5	15
12.	Morally right.	4	11
13.	Responding to needs of workforce.	4	11
14.	Personnel action.	4	11
15.	Equal opportunities department action.	4	11
16.	Better service to customer.	3	9
17.	Staff morale/relationships.	2	5

improving recruitment and retention of staff, and improving staff
morale and relationships in the workforce were added to that figure,
since they could also be said to represent good business sense.

Approximately one-third of organisations said that the legislation
had spurred them to take action while just over a quarter had identified senior management commitment. (The latter figure increases to
over 30 per cent if one includes 'pressure from members' from
some of the local authorities.)

Meanwhile 11 per cent identified good practice and approximately 8 per cent said that it fitted in with the corporate values and
culture to be a fair and caring employer. It is interesting to note that
only 4 per cent said they were doing it because they felt it was
morally right to do so.

It is therefore clear that organisations taking action see positive
benefits from doing so. It is also interesting to see, however, from
the following section how little monitoring takes place to assess
whether these benefits actually accrue.

Monitoring (see Table 5.8)

By far the most common method of monitoring the effectiveness of
actions taken is the examination of workforce profiles, for example
ethnic monitoring, gender monitoring and monitoring of recruitment. (Although promotion was only mentioned specifically by
approximately 5 per cent of organisations it is likely that such
issues could well be monitored as part of general workforce pro-
filing.)

Staff feedback, including attitude surveys, took place in nearly a
quarter of the organisations surveyed. Of all the other types of
monitoring undertaken none was done by more than 10 per cent of
organisations. They included such things as having targets, looking
at turnover and wastage rates, ensuring that such issues are regularly reported at management meetings, and looking at the take-up
of policies (for example the number of job sharers, people working
flexibly and part-timers). Finally, of those organisations who

Table 5.8

Forms of monitoring

		%	n (= 231)
1.	Workforce profiles.	45	104

2.	Monitoring: recruitment
	              promotion
	              training take-up.
		19
		5
		3
			44
			12
			8

3.	Staff feedback (+ consultation groups).	14	32
4.	No monitoring.	11	26
5.	Attitude surveys.	10	22
6.	Complaints and grievances (including harassment).	10	22
7.	Take-up of policies (eg job share, flexible working, part-timers).	8	18
8.	Development of plans/policies/participation in strategies.	8	18
9.	Targets.	5	12
10.	Performance/efficiency/profit/competitiveness.	5	12
11.	Turnover/wastage rates (including graduates, induction).	5	12
12.	Subjective (anecdotal, gut feel, comments).	5	12
13.	Regular reports/management meetings.	5	12
14.	Feedback from other sources (eg unions, customers, community, consultants).	4	9

responded to the question 11 per cent said they did not do any form of monitoring at all.

There are important consequences here for the way a diverse workforce could be managed. If the predominant way of measuring whether initiatives and policies are succeeding is to look at workforce profiles this means that lack of change in the gender and ethnic make-up of the workforce and the distribution of these groups at all levels within the organisation will, by definition, represent failure.

It is not surprising that there is a great emphasis on examining the numbers and type of people employed. After all this is the advice given to organisations by the Equal Opportunities Commission, the Commission for Racial Equality, the Department of Employment and other similar organisations. Yet the limitation of such data if used exclusively as the main source of information in evaluating policies is that success will be defined only in terms of changing the types and numbers of people employed at different levels and in different job categories.

It is also rather surprising how seldom relatively simple data is used, for example on turnover and wastage rates, the number of job sharers and part-time workers, and on people working flexible hours. Such data would obviously give an indication of the take-up of such policies.

Only a minority of organisations carry out any form of staff feedback and attitude survey. In terms of managing a diverse workforce we see this as being a critical ingredient in the development of policies and strategies. An organisation can only respond to the needs of its workforce if it communicates and listens to what its staff feel. It is too often the case that people at the top of the organisation assume they know what the staff or people from particular groups actually want. It is often illuminating to talk to the people concerned and find out what issues they feel they are faced with and how they would like to have them addressed.

There can be little doubt that organisations need to develop a much greater range of indicators to judge their effectiveness in managing diversity. Monitoring data from one's own organisation is important but it should not be used in isolation from other data, nor should it become the only means of determining success.

For example, imagine two recruitment campaigns were carried out, both looking for 10 recruits and both having an equal male/female split in terms of applicants. In one campaign, five men were recruited and five women. In the second campaign, nine men were recruited and only one woman. The question is, which recruitment campaign was fairer? The traditional equal opportunities response would leave us invariably to say that there must be a problem with the second campaign. There can be little doubt that this would be the one most likely to be investigated further for bias. However, it may well be that the first one got the equal balance by unfair means.

Equality of outcome is not therefore necessarily an indicator of the fairness and objectivity of the process. The only way to be confident of the fairness of the processes is to review and audit them thoroughly and regularly, and not to use the outcome statistics as a proxy. It is of some concern therefore to find that none of the organisations indicated that regular reviews of HR processes formed any part of their monitoring. Reviewing, and then reviewing again, the processes operated and the skills of the managers operating them is possibly the most effective way of measuring whether an organisation will manage diversity effectively now and in the future. And yet it appears to be one of the things that is not being monitored at all.

While the business case for managing diversity appears to have been recognised (see Table 5.7), the narrow focus of monitoring casts some doubts on its ability clearly to establish and provide evidence for the claimed benefits. A coherent approach is required where *all* the relevant data is examined. If the reason for taking action is to derive some business benefit then it surely makes sense that the evaluation of the initiatives examines whether the benefit was indeed achieved.

Priority areas for future action

As can be seen from Table 5.9, training has emerged as a priority for over a quarter of the organisations surveyed. Training here was primarily concentrated on people's awareness. If you consider this a form of communication, and if the heading 'communication' was added to training, then approximately 40 per cent of organisations are identifying these as priority areas.

The next series of priority actions is targeted towards specific groups. Approximately a fifth of organisations are going to be taking actions relating to women (eg getting women into management or areas where they are currently underrepresented and taking initiatives

Table 5.9
Priority areas for future action

		%	n (= 148)
1.	Training.	28	41
2.	Actions relating to women (women into management, women into other areas, Opportunity 2000).	19	28
3.	Actions relating to people with disabilities (access, increasing applications).	12	18
4.	Communication.	12	17
5.	Recruitment and selection.	11	16
6.	Positive action.	10	15
7.	Flexible working.	10	15
8.	Actions relating to ethnic minorities (minorities into management, minority applications).	9	13
9.	Harassment.	8	11
10.	Childcare.	7	10

relating to Opportunity 2000). Another 12 per cent of organisations are looking to increase access for people with disabilities and applications from those people. Only 9 per cent of organisations identify actions relating to ethnic minorities as a priority.

This highlights another problem with a traditional equal opportunities response to workplace issues. If actions are addressed to particular groups a hierarchy will develop of those groups that will get priority attention at any particular time. This may lead to frustration and even resentment on the part of those who feel excluded. It also highlights the point that equal opportunities is seen as being about and for women, ethnic minorities and people with disabilities. Nobody mentioned as a priority area getting men into non-traditional areas of work!

Key points

- Communication must be a two-way process; data needs to be fed back to the workforce and the views of both staff and from external sources sought.
- Initiatives relating to the needs of *all* employees rather than of specific groups have been perceived to be more successful ie actions that lead to universal benefit.
- There is scope for organisations to adopt a more flexible approach: initiatives rated as successful, yet infrequently implemented, were those relating to flexibility.
- A coherent approach to evaluation is required; at present a piecemeal approach appears to be prevalent.
- The business case for managing diversity is strongly recognised but is not being evaluated.
- There appears to be an overreliance on workforce profiles as the main means of monitoring. A broader approach is required if the true picture is to be established.
- Future priorities suggest a move away from a traditional equal opportunities approach (ie initiatives targeted towards specific groups). A change in mindset is required away from groups towards a focus on the individual.

6

♟ A Model for Managing Diversity

Many organisations make the mistake of tackling managing diversity by simply providing a series of training sessions. It is not a single issue: managing diversity encompasses the organisation's processes and systems, its culture and the skills of the managers within it.

Trainers are not magicians who can spontaneously turn an organisation around after a one- or two-day course. While training does have a very important role to play in bringing about a diversity-oriented organisation there is a great risk that it is being used as a show-piece to tell the rest of the world: 'Look, we're a diversity-oriented organisation!' If the training is to have the desired impact then the skills, knowledge and perspectives learnt in the session should be easily transferable back to the workplace, a workplace that supports the training with its systems, HR processes and a culture that encourages every employee to reach his or her full potential. Nor should diversity be seen as merely a replacement for the old equal opportunities policy: it must be a corporate value, an integral part of the business strategy, a formal business objective (Harisis and Kleiner 1993).

As John Smale, the CEO of Procter and Gamble, has stated: 'It is important to our future business growth that we find ways to fully capitalise on the diversity of our workforce' (Copeland 1988: 46). Many writers in the diversity field advocate that the philosophy of managing diversity must pervade the entire organisation if diversity is to be managed successfully (McEnrue 1993; Ross and Schneider 1992; Hall and Parker 1993). Managing diversity is not another policy to be added to the multitude of organisational policies: it is an organisational strategy.

The importance of adopting a strategic approach to managing diversity has been stressed by Ross and Schneider (1992). They outline the following reasons:

74

- A firm link is forged with business objectives.
- Senior management commitment and support are established.
- Progress is in line with organisational priorities.
- A coherent approach related to business needs is achieved.
- Problems are anticipated and overcome rather than stumbled upon.
- No one person is responsible for progress.

Indeed, Hammond and Holton (1991) found those organisations that were generally good at managing strategic change were also better than most at managing initiatives related to diversity.

Organisations are themselves realising the benefits of adopting a strategic approach linked to their business needs. Xerox Corporation provides the following three reasons for incorporating its Human Resources Strategic Plan into its business plan (Sessa 1992):

- It moved from being reactive to the business needs to being an integral part of the business plan.
- It encouraged a proactive approach ie forecasting future human resource needs and planning to meet them.
- It fostered the mindset that diversity was an opportunity rather than a threat.

Many authors have presented models of managing diversity – models that aim to guide organisations in their quest to 'fully capitalise on the diversity of [their] workforce'. Implicitly, these models suggest that the ways organisations are currently structured and managed are not suitable for diversity (eg Bowser 1988).

Eleven models for managing diversity have been identified from the literature. Naturally they overlap to a great extent, but no two are identical. Synthesis of the models is quite tricky, however, as some focus entirely on the *process* that should be followed in successfully managing diversity (Cox and Blake 1991; McEnrue 1993; Motwani, Harper, Subramanian and Douglas 1993; Thomas 1990; Rossett and Bickham 1994; Ross and Schneider 1992) while others include a mix of both *process and content* ie the initiatives that should be put in place (Jamieson and O'Mara 1991; Harrington 1993; Thiederman 1994; Bartz *et al.* 1990; Hammond and Kleiner 1992). (See Table 6.1.)

A crude synopsis of the models would indicate the following core process:

1. Audit the current situation: culture, attitudes, systems and procedures.
2. Identify aspects that hinder managing diversity.
3. Implement a strategy to eradicate the hindrances.
4. Continually evaluate progress of the managing diversity strategy.

A validated strategic implementation model

The strategic implementation model for managing diversity presented here is based on our knowledge of the literature and our experience in the area, but more importantly it is as far as we can tell the first to be empirically tested. The validation procedure will be outlined in more detail later in this chapter but first each of the eight elements of the model will be outlined. In doing so, reference will be made, where appropriate, to the 11 models mentioned above and links with their proposed process will be made explicit. A list of indicators for the eight elements will also be presented in the form of questions that you can ask yourself in order to determine whether your organisation is adhering to the model.

The eight elements that make up our model should be looked upon as the range of activities that need to permeate the entire organisation if managing diversity is to be successful.

While the eight elements that make up the model are outlined as separate components, each with its own specific focus, the model itself should not be seen as sequential. Rather, we would expect to see one or more of the elements being actioned at any one time throughout the organisation. In fact the model could be likened to a spider's web, where it is impossible to touch one strand without having a simultaneous impact on all the other strands that make up the web. (See Figure 6.1.)

Figure 6.1
The strategy web

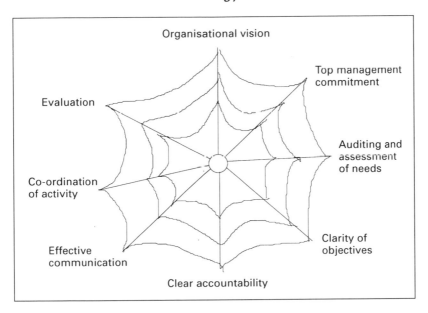

Organisational vision

If diversity is to become a business issue then the organisation must have a clear vision of what it intends to achieve and why this vision is important (Harrington 1993; Thomas 1990; Rossett and Bickham 1994; Ross and Schneider 1992). The message must be clearly communicated that diversity is being actively pursued as a business objective.

Thomas (1990: 114) claims that the vision an organisation needs to communicate is one of fully harnessing the needs of every employee. In Thomas's opinion this image is necessary as it focuses on individual potential rather than equality, and in doing so the vision 'ignores the tensions of coexistence, plays down the

Table 6.1
Models of managing diversity

Process models of managing diversity	Process and content models of managing diversity
Thomas (1990)	**Jamieson and O'Mara (1991)**

• Clarify your motivation.
• Clarify your vision.
• Expand your focus.
• Audit your corporate culture.
• Modify your assumptions.
• Modify your systems.
• Modify your models.
• Help your people pioneer.
• Apply the special considerations test.
• Continue affirmative action.
	• Matching people and jobs:
	  – individualise job profiles, assessment methods, orientation, careers
	  – assess individual strengths and weaknesses
	  – review and change key HRC processes.
	
	• Matching and rewarding performance:
	  – examine different ways of work planning, motivating and rewarding mentoring, coaching, feedback
	  – flexibility of approach in dealing with appraisal, development.

McEnrue (1993)	• Informing and involving people:
	  – keep people informed
	  – use flexible systems eg ongoing and temporary groups
	  – suggestion schemes, attitude surveys, focus groups.

• The role of top management.
• Identifying needs.
• Methods of managing diversity: use of customised methods.
• Scope and time-frame of efforts: realistic expectation of scope and time-frames.
• Required skills: skills development.
• Measuring progress: establish controls tied to business results.
	• Supporting lifestyle and life needs:
	  – identify people's needs and interests, and create supportive options eg childcare, work hours, leave options
	  – new benefits policies
	  – special interest networks
	  – supportive and creative managers.

Cox and Blake (1991)	**Bartz et al. (1990)**
• Leadership: enlist top management support and commitment. • Training: managing and valuing diversity training. • Research: collecting information pertaining to diversity-related issues. • Analysis and change of culture and human resource management systems. • Follow-up: conduct analyses of change of culture and HRM system.	• Organisational acceptance and commitment. • Understanding the concept of diversity and attributes of major subpopulations. • Identify workstyles and motivation. • Developmental needs and career aspirations. • Personal needs, including flexible working.

Table 6.1
continued

Process models of managing diversity	Process and content models of managing diversity
Motwani et al. (1993) • Assessment. • Planning. • Programming. • Implementation. • Evaluation. **Rossett and Bickham (1994)** • Link diversity with business priorities. • Top management support. • Specify acceptable/unacceptable behaviours. • Role models. • Communication. • Measure results. **Ross and Schneider (1992)** • Diagnosis. • Setting aims. • Spreading ownership. • Policy development. • Training.	**Hammond and Kleiner (1992)** • Acknowledge differences of the workplace. • Examine policies and procedures – eliminate areas of bias or discrimination. • Conduct a needs assessment. • Develop training programmes. • Communication: ensure management proves its commitment and openness by follow-up. • Be constantly aware of cultural differences and biases. **Thiederman (1994)** • Organisational soul-searching. • Accountability. • Senior management involvement. • Communication. • Create hospitable workplace. • Adjust strategies and processes. • Set up special interest groups. • Measure results. **Harrington (1993)** • Top management support and commitment. • Open attitude to new ways of working. • Distinguish between three approaches to managing diversity. • Audit your workforce and customers. • Create a vision. • Training in managing diversity awareness. • Be flexible. • Skills training. • Help reduce work–family conflicts.

uncomfortable realities of difference. The vision should encapsulate the principles of managing diversity, communicating a shared
vision of where the organisation is going and the expected rewards.
The vision can then be made explicit in the form of a policy or even
a directive outlining the main areas of attention.

It is important that time and careful consideration are given to
formulating the policy. Too often organisations find themselves with
an unclear policy that does more to confuse staff than communicate
to them the intentions and commitment of the organisation. The
links with the business objectives must be made explicit in the
policy. If managing diversity is to be accepted as an organisation-
wide concern then the vision and policy must be seen actively to
support the business goals. This is of value not only in ensuring the
acceptance of diversity as an organisational strategy but also in
enabling its ultimate success (Holland 1988).

Clear indication should be given how this policy is to be used by
various parts of the organisation, whom it affects and the benefits to
be obtained. It is our opinion (as we hope should now be clear) that
individuals, not groups, should be the focus of both the vision and
the policy. Some organisations, though seeing themselves as managers of diversity, still make the mistake of highlighting specific
groups in their communication. This serves both to alienate individuals who do not fall into these groups and to send mixed signals

Table 6.2

Is there an organisational vision?

- Has the organisation made a clear statement outlining why
  managing diversity is important to the business?
- Has the organisation made a clear statement of the expected
  outcomes of the managing diversity strategy?
- Are the organisational aims for managing diversity apparent
  from the policy?
- Do the business needs of the organisation feature in the
  policy?
- Does the policy outline specific requirements in terms of
  implementation?
- Has a statement referring to managing diversity been built
  into the overall organisational mission?

whether it is traditional equal opportunities or managing diversity that is the organisational goal. The focus on individuals and on achieving everyone's full potential must therefore be made explicit (Ross and Schneider 1992; Thomas 1990). Managing diversity is the responsibility of *all* employees.

Top management commitment

A number of models have emphasised the critical importance of establishing senior management support and commitment (McEnrue 1993; Cox and Blake 1991; Bartz *et al.* 1990; Hammond and Kleiner 1992; Thiederman 1994; Harrington 1993; Rossett and Bickham 1994).

McEnrue (1993), in outlining her model for managing diversity, presents the following three reasons for gaining commitment from the top:

- It communicates a vision that motivates employees by focusing their energy on a common goal.
- Only top management are in a position to ensure that all the initiatives concerning key management processes – eg recruitment, selection, induction, appraisal, promotion – are initiated, co-ordinated and monitored.
- A commitment of time and resources is required, and this commitment will often need to be sanctioned by top management.

As the benefits to be gained from managing diversity are increasingly recognised more and more top managers will see it as a business imperative rather than simply the 'right thing' to do.

Research by Towers Perrin in the USA suggests that gaining this support may not be an uphill struggle. Their survey of human resource managers in 200 organisations in 1990/1 resulted in a report entitled *Workforce 2000 Today: A bottom-line concern*. This report indicated that 54 per cent of respondents suggested that management support had increased, with 95 per cent attributing this increase to greater awareness and 89 per cent to the need to attract and retain a skilled workforce. In our own research, discussed in

Chapter 5, the commitment of top management was one of the main reasons why organisations had taken action.

Cox and Blake (1991: 52) strongly affirm this commitment must go beyond 'sloganism'. They suggest this is achieved when:

- human, financial and technical resources are being provided
- managing diversity is included in the corporate strategy and is a regular topic at senior-level meetings
- there is a willingness to change human resource management systems
- there is a willingness to commit energy and resources to a long-term project rather than a short-term fix.

Senior management commitment needs to be visible, active and ongoing. Employees need to be aware of the commitment: it must be clearly communicated not only in writing but also in actions. Indeed if senior management are to be seen to be committed to this process then they must ensure that they themselves monitor, evaluate and, if necessary, modify their *own* behaviour. For example, Levi Strauss firmly established management commitment by having senior management undergo the diversity training and then take the lead in cascading the training down through the organisation (Thiederman 1994).

Table 6.3
Do you have top management commitment?

- Do senior management actively participate in the implementation of diversity?
- Are all employees fully aware of the support and commitment of top management?
- Do all staff agree that management are fully committed?
- Is the commitment stated by senior management reflected in their actions?
- Have senior management supported their stated commitment with the allocation of adequate resources?

Auditing and assessment of needs

When setting out to manage diversity a first step is to take a good look at your organisation in terms of its culture, the systems and procedures in operation and the make-up of your human resources. This requires the collection of data and the auditing of the key management processes.

The majority of the models advocate the crucial importance of conducting a managing diversity health check on the organisation (McEnrue 1993; Cox and Blake 1991; Thiederman 1994; Bartz *et al.* 1990; Ross and Schneider 1992; Motwani *et al.* 1993; Harrington 1993; Hammond and Kleiner 1992). The aim is to uncover sources of potential bias and ways in which the organisational culture, structure and processes can overtly and covertly discriminate against certain individuals. The data collection process must be rigorous, as the data uncovered will form the basis of defining the objectives for the implementation of the strategy. However, it is important to note that the auditing and assessing element of the model is an ongoing activity, not a discrete first stage. The data uncovered provides both a starting-point and a baseline against which to measure progress.

Cox and Blake (1991) state this research stage is necessary for the following reasons:

- It identifies issues to be addressed in diversity awareness training.
- It identifies areas where changes are needed and gives suggestions on how to make them.
- It provides useful baseline data for the evaluation stage.

Another advantage of information gathering is that the involvement of employees at this early stage not only elicits valuable information for the formulation of objectives but it also spreads ownership of the managing diversity strategy to the entire workforce.

In conducting the health check, data needs to be collected on the following:

- the human resource systems: selection, induction, appraisal and promotion
- the attitudes and opinions of employees
- profile data: age profiles and figures showing the numbers of women, men and ethnic minorities employed and their location in the organisation.

The following methods could be employed:

- attitude surveys
- feedback from focus groups/group discussions
- task group feedback
- interviews
- questionnaires
- analysis of personnel indices: selection ratios, turnover rates, performance appraisal ratings, promotion ratings, and training allocation.

The need to ensure that the human resource systems are fair to everyone and that they are operated fairly is examined more closely in Chapter 8. These processes need to be audited. Three critical aspects to be examined are:

- the criteria employed
- how the criteria are assessed
- the skills of the managers operating the systems.

In his model Thomas (1990) advocates using what he calls the Special Consideration Test, that is, examining processes to see whether some groups are advantaged by their operation. If this is found to be the case, the processes need to be reviewed. The Special Consideration Test applies equally to instances where women and minorities are the ones who appear to be gaining from the processes.

It is not only the processes and systems in an organisation that can stifle diversity; the organisational culture may also hinder it in terms of what it implies are acceptable attitudes, approaches, styles or behaviour. The culture may not only be resistant to managing diversity but it may also conflict with the fundamental principles underpinning diversity. A culture audit must therefore be conducted in order to unravel these tacit assumptions and values, and to identify ways in which the culture may inadvertently put people at a disadvantage. The audit can be conducted via a climate survey, interviews and/or group discussions with a random sample of employees from all levels of the organisation.

In carrying out a culture audit it is necessary to question perceptions of the written and unwritten rules regarding promotion, training, career development, work allocation, and formal/informal feedback on performance. Ideas should also be solicited from employees on how to do things better.

Table 6.4
Are you auditing and assessing organisational needs?

– Are existing human resource systems audited and re-audited to ensure their fairness to everyone?
– Have the opinions of the workforce been canvassed with regard to managing diversity?
– Are employees encouraged to volunteer their opinions and ideas regarding managing diversity?
– Has a study of the corporate culture and climate for diversity been conducted?
– Has the organisational profile been examined to establish the breadth of the diversity in the workforce and the spread across the hierarchy?

Clarity of objectives

Having identified the areas that require attention it is necessary to establish the objectives for implementation (McEnrue 1993; Cox and Blake 1991; Hammond and Kleiner 1992; Motwani *et al.* 1993; Ross and Schneider 1992).

A coherent strategy must have clear, quantifiable objectives with set time-scales. Only then can progress be measured and reviewed in a consistent fashion. It is important however that these objectives are not seen as quotas or targets that are set in stone. This risk can be overcome by the way objectives are worded, communicated and measured. Thomas (1990) highlighted the importance of 'helping your people pioneer' ie recognising that managing diversity is a change process and that there is no one right way to manage it. In this way objectives should be seen as indicators or benchmarks rather than targets to be reached whatever the cost.

The objectives could include for example conducting an audit of the organisation or reviewing recruitment and selection procedures, training key people in diversity or conducting an attitude survey. The objectives do not need to relate to numbers of people in particular jobs. If they did, they would be contradictory to the approach we are advocating.

Objectives and action plans reinforce a strategic approach where ownership is organisation-wide. Given that the objectives are based on the information gathered from the workforce, a strong sense of support and commitment to the objectives should result. This support will be strengthened through effective communication of the objectives.

It is vital that these objectives are seen as an integral part of the business needs. McEnrue (1993) claims that the objectives should be linked to business results, for example new product development or customer service. Ross and Schneider (1992) assert that the establishment of clear objectives ensures a proactive rather than a reactive approach and helps sustain momentum. According to McEnrue (1993), objectives also make it possible to show improvement and demonstrate progress. She argues that this increases the confidence of the workforce. This increased confidence is then

Table 6.5
Do you have clear objectives?

- Have clear, quantifiable objectives been specified for managing diversity?
- Have the objectives been developed in conjunction with the business objectives?
- Has a programme of managing-diversity-related action been generated?
- Have the managing diversity actions been prioritised according to present needs?

likely to enhance the chances of achieving results, as employees will be reassured that managing diversity is not simply another flavour of the month.

Clear accountability

Once actions have been initiated accountability must be established. If diversity is to be implemented effectively the diversity policies and strategies need to be properly understood by people within the organisation. There must be key people at all levels of the organisation who will support and guide the change. Traditionally these people have invariably been human resource professionals, but they should not hold exclusive responsibility for managing diversity.

Accountability must extend across the entire organisation. Every employee should not only be aware of what is required of them but they should also be accountable for their responsibilities in the implementation of initiatives. Cox and Blake (1991) advocate the importance of accountability and claim that managing diversity should be no different from any other business activity.

It is not only individuals that should be accountable but also the organisational systems and processes that are in operation. It has often been the case that the selection or promotion processes in an organisation are subtly discriminatory against particular types of people. This discrimination is not necessarily intentional; in fact it is often so embedded in the organisational practices that it is accepted as legitimate. Accountability of the systems ensures that these processes are continually modified and assessed to check they are operating fairly, in line with the principles of managing diversity. The managers running the systems and processes will therefore ultimately be accountable for their fair operation.

One way of establishing accountability highlighted in the literature is to reward managers according to their diversity efforts (Greenslade 1991). However, this form of accountability needs to be managed properly or it may create more problems than it solves. One potential problem was highlighted by McEnrue (1993). In an organisation that she surveyed managers were rewarded according to their success in recruiting employees from minority groups. But this incentive alone resulted in a 'revolving door' (McEnrue 1993: 25): the turnover rate was ultimately found to be higher amongst minority-group employees as there was no incentive for the managers to keep them. This is also highlighted in our example of the engineering organisation cited in Chapter 9 (see Table 9.3), where the recruiters saw the advantages of taking on more women because of the priorities communicated to them but saw little kudos in employing more minorities.

Another unintended consequence may be that managers will get hooked on the quantity of diversity initiatives they are involved in rather than the quality of their contribution. There is obviously a fine line to be walked between focusing managers' attention on particular issues and still maintaining their awareness of the broader picture.

In our view *managers should be rewarded for their ability both to develop themselves and their employees*. It is this optimisation of all the human potential within the organisation that is crucial to managing diversity successfully, not how many men or women are recruited or how many initiatives have been set in motion.

Table 6.6
Accountability

- Are specific guidelines outlined to employees of their role in managing diversity?
- Are managers assessed according to their ability to develop themselves and their employees?
- Is managing diversity perceived as an organisation-wide priority?
- Have the human resource systems been modified according to managing diversity principles?

Effective communication

It almost goes without saying that if managing diversity is an organisation-wide strategy then all information regarding progress must be shared throughout the organisation. To be effective this communication must first ensure that all employees have a full understanding of the issues, the organisational vision and the benefits to be gained. The next step is to keep staff continually updated on progress and, most importantly, to solicit feedback from them on how to proceed.

Soliciting feedback is crucially important not only to ensure new ideas are harnessed but also to serve as a motivator for staff. Communication on progress to all employees also serves to enhance confidence in senior management commitment and will go a long way to reduce scepticism that diversity is just another initiative, a flavour of the month, that will go nowhere.

Ross and Schneider (1992: 65) place great emphasis on the need to spread ownership. They suggest that by involving everyone in the organisation it is possible to ensure that managing diversity enters the 'organisational bloodstream' and that this will result in actual behavioural changes rather than mere lip-service.

Communication is necessary both within the organisation and with the outside world. It is interesting to note that only Thiederman (1994) highlights communicating your commitment to the market-place as an important aspect of a managing diversity model. The remaining models view communication as an internal issue, and yet communication with the public, clients and customers is perhaps also an important component. An organisation's commitment to diversity should be clearly communicated to the outside world via advertisements, brochures, and conferences.

American Express, in their quest to manage diversity, developed a strategy for communicating their vision of 'becoming the best place to work' to their employees. The strategy consisted of the formation of a Communications Task Force to develop the communication plan. By soliciting feedback from a focus group they ensured their communication was timely, clear and ultimately received and understood (Morrison and Herlihy 1992).

A number of communication channels should be used to ensure messages are consistently and clearly communicated to everyone: for example publications, reports, one-to-one feedback, formation of focus groups etc. Many of the models advocate running workshops and training courses specifically for managing diversity

(Thiederman 1994; Ross and Schneider 1992; Cox and Blake 1991; Hammond and Kleiner 1992; Harrington 1993; Rossett and Bickham 1994). Essentially this training takes one of two forms:

- diversity awareness training
- diversity skills training.

While we believe that both these forms of training have a valuable role to play in the communication process, we have serious reservations about the content that some writers advocate. We see training as a means of both communicating the principles of managing diversity – why and how it is important to the business objectives – and of equipping managers with the skills they need to ensure that they are developing everyone to their full potential.

Training can also foster two-way communication, where employees can air their views and express their needs. As a result expectations will be raised and it will be necessary to communicate continuously, updating everyone on how their suggestions were actioned. Some models, however, advocate carrying out training that educates participants on the 'differences' between groups and how to respond to them effectively. It is our belief that this type of training is inappropriate and out of line with the values of managing diversity.

The content of training courses will be discussed in more detail in Chapter 10. However, some further elaboration is appropriate here.

What many of these training courses are setting out to achieve is to teach managers that they must, in the words of Heather McDonald (1993: 25), 'judge individual behaviour as an expression of racial, sexual and cultural difference; on the other [hand], they are told that they must not base their behaviour on how they think members of a particular cultural group will react'.

There is a danger that diversity training focused on groups will reinforce existing stereotypes or even create new ones. Indeed McDonald (1993) suggests that these courses actually *advocate* stereotyping as long as it is the right sort ie the diversity kind, for example the idea that 'women are better at building successful work relationships'. An example may be useful here. It has been noted that in some training sessions of this kind trainers make an example of their trainees. A training course reported by McDonald (1993) describes a session where a female trainee was asked to stand up as a member of the 'privileged white élite'. The trainer continued to focus on this woman throughout the session with the result that she was in tears by the end. Is this a necessary stage on the way to 'tapping into the potential of all your employees'? We doubt it.

Table 6.7
Are you communicating with all staff?

- Are all staff aware of the organisational vision for managing diversity?
- Has the policy been distributed to all employees?
- Has the organisation promoted its commitment to manage diversity outside the organisation?
- Is information on progress regularly fed back to all employees?
- Is feedback solicited from the workforce on how to proceed?
- Have employees received training on why managing diversity is important to the organisation?
- Have employees received training on how to manage diversity effectively?
- Have managers been trained how to develop both themselves and their staff so that their full potential is realised?

Co-ordination of activity

While top management commitment is essential, the implementation of the strategy needs to be co-ordinated either by individuals or groups at all levels of the organisation.

Large organisations such as Grand Metropolitan (in some of their subsidiaries) and Motorola have developed positions such as Vice-President Diversity or Diversity Director. These individuals have overall responsibility for ensuring that diversity is effectively managed. It may not be necessary in a small organisation to have someone working full time but it is important that a co-ordinator role be established for the efficient implementation of the strategy.

Such a co-ordinator needs to examine what is happening elsewhere within the organisation and beyond to see if there are other actions being taken that could be learned from.

Ross and Schneider (1992) propose that individual departments be given some autonomy in developing their own initiatives. Co-ordination will see to it that lessons are learnt and shared with other areas: in this way consistency is ensured. Lessons can also be learnt from other organisations. Information on valuable practices may be gleaned and routes to avoid highlighted. However, as McEnrue (1993) has pointed out, each organisation is unique and while they should learn from the experiences of others it is crucial that they develop their own customised approach.

Cox and Blake (1991) and Harisis and Kleiner (1993) feel that 'diversity champions' are needed especially at lower organisational levels to ensure cross-functional and hierarchical involvement. They also advocate involvement of a diversity task force in addition to the employment of someone specifically in a diversity role. These task forces are usually headed by someone senior but also include representatives from other parts of the organisation. Their role is to solicit opinions about the current situation and to highlight areas for improvement and areas of good practice. Champions should be known throughout the organisation and their role clearly communicated to emphasise that they are not responsible solely for managing diversity but rather for managing it effectively and smoothly.

Table 6.8
Is the managing diversity strategy co-ordinated?

- Have 'champions' of diversity been appointed?
- Are there 'champions' at all levels of the organisation?
- Has the role of these 'champions' been clearly communicated to everyone?
- Is regular contact maintained between departments concerning progress on diversity issues?
- Has contact been made outside the organisation in order to learn from others about diversity?

Evaluation

Evaluation is a crucial element of any change-initiative (Cox and Blake 1991; Thiederman 1994; Rossett and Bickham 1994; Motwani *et al.* 1993). It should be regarded as an ongoing process, constantly reviewing progress of the managing diversity strategy towards the realisation of the vision. Rigorous evaluation is essential to make the strategy and the initiatives effective. Continuous evaluation also ensures that information is fed back on an ongoing basis. This information can be acted upon quickly in order to realign actions or initiatives where necessary.

The evaluation stage necessitates reference back to both the vision and the objectives. Thus it is crucial to have produced these with clarity. Futhermore, the auditing process should have given some baseline data against which comparisons could be made, for example turnover rates, selection ratios and attitudes.

The information gathered during the evaluation should not be retained by management; rather, if diversity is to be the responsibility of all employees, then they too should receive this information. Information on progress will serve as a reminder of the importance of diversity and may also elicit feedback from staff on how to proceed.

Table 6.9
Is progress being evaluated?

- Has a system of in-depth evaluation been put in place?
- Is progress measured against predetermined objectives?
- Is this evaluation an ongoing process?
- Are the results of the evaluation fed back to all employees?

Validation of the model

While many models of implementation have been outlined it is surprising to find that no attempts have been made to test them empirically. Many, if not all, are based on case studies, anecdotal evidence or past experience.

Research on our strategic implementation model has presented evidence that organisations who follow the proposed elements are more successful in implementing diversity initiatives. Details of this research and the results are described in this section.

The aim of the research was to explore the relationship between the diversity implementation model and successful implementation of managing diversity initiatives. The hypothesis we wished to test is shown below.

The Hypothesis

The degree of success of an organisation in terms of implementing managing diversity will be positively related to the eight process elements outlined in our strategic implementation model.

The data to test this hypothesis came from two surveys: the first examined 'content' (ie the initiatives implemented), and the results of this survey were presented in Chapter 5. The second focused on the 'process' of implementation. The nature of these surveys and the method employed to calculate success are outlined below.

Content survey

As described in Chapter 5 Pearn Kandola carried out a large-scale study of 285 organisations examining the initiatives that they had put in place to manage diversity. A total of 40 initiatives were listed in the questionnaire. A sample of the initiatives is listed in Table 6.10. Each participating organisation was asked not only to indicate which initiatives they had in place but also how successful they believed them to be.

Table 6.10
Sample initiatives from the content survey

- Giving fair selection training to recruiters.
- Allowing staff to take career breaks.
- Eliminating age criteria from selection decisions.
- Introducing equal rights and benefits for part-time workers.

Process survey

Whereas the first survey focused on the content aspects of implementing managing diversity, our managing diversity model outlined above focused on process issues. We wanted to discover whether it was possible to differentiate, by using our model, between organisations that had implemented initiatives most successfully and those that had been least successful.

In order to examine the model in relation to the content data a further survey was conducted. A second questionnaire was constructed, based on our strategic model of implementing managing diversity. It contained eight scales relating to each of the elements, with a total of 18 subscales. Table 6.11 contains sample items of the scale relating to 'communication'. This questionnaire was sent to organisations that had completed the content survey and indicated they were willing to take part in a follow-up questionnaire. Information was collected from 49 organisations through a postal survey.

Table 6.11
Sample items of 'communication'

- Managing diversity progress is regularly fed back to employees.
- Employees have received training to equip them with the relevant skills to manage diversity.
- The organisation has promoted its image as a diversity-oriented employer outside the organisation.

Determining the success rating. The hypothesis relates to the impact of the model on *successful* implementation of managing diversity initiatives. A method of determining success was therefore necessary.

The content survey provided one source of information on success, as respondents were asked to rate the perceived success of each initiative. Therefore a measure of success for each organisation could be established by calculating their *average perceived success rating* across all the initiatives rated. However, because of the subjective nature of this rating, it was considered inappropriate to use it in isolation. A more objective method of measuring success was developed by taking both quality and quantity into consideration. Quality was established by asking five experts in the managing diversity field to rate the importance of each initiative for the effective management of diversity. The ratings given to each initiative were then used as a quantitative weighting for each initiative. The *final success score* for the implementation of managing diversity was thus calculated by obtaining the sum of these weighted ratings.

The problems inherent in defining success did not go unrecognised. In an ideal world we would have liked the opportunity to base our definition on in-depth qualitative analysis of the organisations concerned. However, we feel that the measure devised was the most sensitive given the data available.

(Note: Of the 40 initiatives in the content survey, only a subset of 24 were selected for use in the validation research. The rationale for this selection was that some initiatives in the original survey related to process issues (eg having a policy or a strategy) and were therefore also covered in the second survey. Inclusion of these initiatives would therefore have artificially inflated the correlations obtained. Excluding the duplicated items meant we were being conservative in the use of the data.)

Testing the hypothesis

The hypothesis was tested by examining, for the 49 organisations, the relationship between the score obtained on each of the eight elements of the model and the *final success score for implementing managing diversity*. Correlations were used to establish the relationships.

A statistically significant correlation was found between each of the eight factors and the success score for the implementation of managing diversity. Moreover the total score produced by adding up the scores from the eight elements also correlated significantly with organisational success in implementing managing diversity. The specific findings are outlined in Table 6.12.

What this means is that organisations which follow the processes outlined in our model should have a greater chance of having a *genuinely strategic approach* to managing diversity and of being successful with it.

Table 6.12
Summary of results

The degree of success of the organisation in implementing managing diversity was found to be positively related to:

1. The clarity of the organisational vision
   ($r=0.42$, $p=0.002$, one-tailed significance)
2. The extent of top management commitment
   ($r=0.39$, $p=0.004$, one-tailed-significance)
3. The auditing and assessing of needs
   ($r=0.53$, $p=0.000$, one-tailed significance)
4. The setting of clear objectives
   ($r=0.52$, $p=0.000$, one-tailed significance)
5. The degree of accountability
   ($r=0.27$, $p=0.042$, one-tailed significance)
6. The degree of communication within the organisation
   ($r=0.26$, $p=0.039$, one-tailed significance)
7. The extent of co-ordination
   ($r=0.30$, $p=0.023$, one-tailed significance)
8. The degree to which the strategy and actions are evaluated
   ($r=0.52$, $p=0.000$, one-tailed significance)

Conclusion

Many models of managing diversity seem to be based more on personal experience and anecdote than on anything objective. There are definitely valuable lessons to be learnt from personal experience and indeed it is essential these lessons are communicated to others who may be embarking on a similar course. It is only through sharing these experiences that we will learn from them.

However, the research suggests that our strategic diversity implementation model is the first ever to have been empirically tested and validated. In other words, the following have all been found to be positively related to the successful strategic implementation of managing diversity:

- having a clear vision
- having senior management support
- auditing your needs
- setting objectives
- communicating with your workforce
- establishing accountability
- co-ordinating the actions
- evaluating the outcomes.

Validation and verification of the diversity models are necessary and important. Such validation is not only of academic interest but will also provide useful data for the many organisations grappling with the concept of managing diversity. These organisations need to be sure that they have a valid, secure framework within which to build their strategies and this model should provide them with a good starting-point at the very least.

The IDV experience

International Distillers and Vintners (IDV) is one organisation concerned about managing diversity and their approach will be outlined as a mini case-study. IDV are one of the few organisations in the UK committed to managing diversity rather than equal opportunities. It is early days for IDV but their strategic approach, which incorporates many of the elements of the strategic implementation model, has very positive signs.

In constructing its mission (Table 6.13) IDV included the elements it considered to be important to its long-term profitability. These included, as can be seen, a commitment to diversity and the advantages it offers. Such a message sends clear signals to staff about what the organisation considers to be important and the way it expects to conduct business.

The code of business conduct (see Table 6.14) at IDV contains specific and explicit reference to discrimination. It also places the

Table 6.13

The IDV mission

Our mission is to ensure that:

- IDV will be closer to its customers, to consumers and to the heart of the market
- IDV will have the strongest portfolio of value-added brands, which will always be competitive within their markets
- IDV people will be high-calibre, responding to professional leadership, stimulating challenges and individual opportunities, with realistic rewards to match
- **IDV will value the diversity contained within its global workforce and build these differences into a corporate strength** (authors' emphasis)
- IDV will exercise the leadership role to strengthen the communities in which it is active and conduct its business in a socially responsible manner.

---

emphasis on individuals, not groups, for the way people should be treated, stressing that processes should be fair and objective. In addition the organisation recognises the importance of having an effective appraisal system and is auditing this to ensure it is working fairly and objectively.

In order to make people aware of the issues relating to diversity, a senior management training programme was undertaken which included the chief executive and the whole of the IDV board. Over 200 senior management staff also went through this two-day programme. (The objectives and outcomes of the top management training are presented in Table 6.15.) The workshops were used to explore diversity and to see whether it had any relevance to the organisation. They were also used to gain feedback from senior management about what should be done next and, indeed, what should *not* be done. These workshops have also been run for managing directors and HR directors of IDV's various European operations.

Table 6.14

Sections from the IDV code of business conduct

Discrimination

– The recognition and encouragement of the uniqueness of individual contributions within a team environment is the embodiment of our employment policy.

  This ensures that in all aspects of employment such as recruitment, compensation, training, promotion, transfer, termination and benefits, all employees will be treated as individuals solely according to their abilities to meet job requirements without regard to factors such as race, religion, colour, ethnic or national origin, age, disability, gender, marital status or sexual preference.

Harassment

– Harassment of any kind, such as racial or sexual harassment, is completely unacceptable within IDV companies, and it is the responsibility of Board Directors to put appropriate policies and procedures in place to address it.

Political conduct

– IDV dissociates itself from any political activity which incites extremism or challenges our commitment to cultural diversity and equal opportunities.

Table 6.15

Objectives and outcomes for top management diversity training within IDV

I OBJECTIVES

1. To examine the business case for valuing diversity.
2. To develop an understanding of diversity in general and managing diversity within IDV in particular.
3. To examine whether or not this is an issue for IDV.
4. To decide on actions, if any, to be taken.

II OUTCOMES

– A shared understanding of the issues.
– A prioritisation of action areas which will give highest returns.
– To enable direction to be given to our organisation to deliver the agreed results in this area.
– An understanding that this is a strategic issue which will impact on the direction of our business.

The issue of diversity is not seen as standing alone – isolated from the rest of the business. Instead it is seen as something that should run through other policies and processes. In the organisation's vision and principles other aspects of diversity are mentioned, for example 'good ideas can come from anyone, anywhere in IDV'; and 'IDV managers ensure that individual contribution to the overall success of the team is maximised and recognised'. Documents referring to the building of new brands also contain references to diversity, for example: 'successful partnerships are built upon mutual respect and the ability to listen to, understand and benefit from other people's points of view and experience', and 'we actively encourage diversity and skills, experience and personalities within the team'.

Having diversity presented in different documents in different ways and by stressing the business benefit ensures there is a greater probability that people will not only receive the message but also absorb and accept it.

Key points

- Adopting a strategic approach to managing diversity is crucial to its success.
- Our eight-element strategic implementation model is presented:
  - organisational vision
  - top management commitment
  - auditing and assessment of needs
  - clarity of objectives
  - clear accountability
  - effective communication
  - co-ordination of activity
    evaluation.
- As far as we know ours is *the first-ever validated model* for implementing managing diversity; organisations following the processes outlined in the model were found to be successful in the implementation of managing diversity initiatives.
- The IDV experience is provided as a mini case-study of an organisation moving along the diversity as opposed to the equality route.

7

♟ A Diversity Competence: the Role of the Individual

An area that has received increasing attention is the role of individual managers and the skills they need to manage a diverse workforce. In order to appreciate the skills required it is necessary to understand the issues that minorities face at work; these are discussed in the first section of this chapter.

Another issue central to managing diversity is stereotyping and the way it can affect how managers view and treat their staff, and how team members relate to one another. The second section of this chapter therefore examines stereotypes – what they are and how they can affect people's judgements of others. In the third section we present some attempts to define a diversity competence, relate these to other definitions of a communication competence and look at the similarities between them.

Finally we look at what individual managers can do to improve their approaches to managing a diverse workforce.

Being in a minority

Barnouw (1969) felt that there was ethnocentrism in all aspects of society, including work. As the workforce changes ethnocentrism may become exacerbated; this can then cause difficulties with relationships. Brown (1983) stated that minorities are often more sensitive to discriminatory patterns within organisations. Those in the majority, however, are relatively unaware of them and may feel vulnerable, insulted and perhaps even threatened by claims and accusations made by minorities. This can escalate to such an extent that the person who raises the concern is labelled a troublemaker who cannot work as part of a team, who has a chip on their shoulder and so on.

It is important to recognise that people can be in a minority for many reasons and not only because of race, sex or disability. Feelings of vulnerability, self-consciousness, anger, intimidation etc can be experienced by anyone and may be caused by class, status in the organisation, language, background – even the food they eat. In short, most of us know what it feels like to be in a minority at some time or another.

Kanter (1977) identified three issues that minorities face in the workplace:

- Certain behaviours, particularly those related to poor performance, are noticed more readily than for those in the majority.
- There is a tendency to focus on areas of difference between groups and to magnify and exaggerate them: the differences therefore become larger than they really are.
- Behaviour is misinterpreted or misattributed, which then enables people to maintain their stereotypes.

Similarly, Gordon, DiTomaso and Farris (1991), in a study conducted amongst scientists in the research and development arm of an organisation, found that women and minorities reported what they referred to as an 'invisibility' syndrome. This meant, for example, that during a meeting an idea of theirs would be ignored, yet when the same idea was brought up later by a white male it was often adopted by the group.

When people in the majority fail to respond in a fair and open-minded way to the concerns brought to their attention by people in a minority they are essentially saying that the problem is not important or that it may lie with the person who brought the complaint in the first place. For example, until recently it had been relatively easy to ignore issues of sexual harassment because it was felt that some women were being oversensitive.

The other consequence of not being responsive to the concerns of minorities is that it reduces the responsibility of the majority to review, reconsider and perhaps even change their behaviour. In effect, people in the majority are minimising their chances of learning from the experience of the minority and of making the organisational culture one in which everyone can feel comfortable and make an effective contribution. As Cox (1992: 142) states: 'A primary reason that we have failed to capitalise on the richness of diversity in our workforce is that learning is often one-way. The new recruit learns how to fit into the organisation, but what is the organisation willing to learn from the new recruit?' And, as he goes on to say, 'adaptation and flexibility should be a two-way street'.

Stereotyping

An ever-present issue and one of the biggest obstacles in managing diversity is stereotyping. Managing a diverse workforce can often be a difficult task not necessarily because of the real differences that exist between people but because of those that we *believe* exist.

People entering organisations bring their own assumptions and preconceptions, and they use these ideas to form new impressions about other groups in the organisation and in society. If we base our actions towards an individual on our assumptions about the group to which they belong we are engaging in stereotypical behaviour. The *Dictionary of Personality and Social Psychology* (Harré and Lamb 1983: 347) states that stereotypes are:

> Usually considered to be oversimplified, rigid, and generalised beliefs about groups of people in which all individuals from the same group are regarded as having the same set of leading characteristics. Stereotypes of members of a national, religious or racial group may affect the impressions people form of individuals who are identifiable members of that group.

Stereotypes abound in society and these are obviously carried into the workplace. Several researchers have identified the characteristics usually associated with men and women or with masculinity and femininity, for example Capra (1983). Other research, for example Powell (1988), has also shown that the characteristics of a 'good' manager matched up more closely with the supposedly male characteristics than the supposedly female ones. Adherence to stereotypes will, and obviously does, lead to certain groups being treated differently from others.

This prejudice also prevails in matters of race. This has been illustrated in a study by Gordon *et al.* (1991) who interviewed a range of people within organisations about the pressures and issues they faced. One complaint from black people in particular was that even after completing a comprehensive selection procedure and possessing the necessary job credentials their competence was still frequently questioned. Women felt management questioned their commitment to their careers because childcare responsibilities made it difficult for them to put in the extra hours needed for the most challenging assignments.

Braham (1989) offers the view that managers need to be aware of the presumption of competence, which in most cases will mean that white males (typically) are presumed to be competent unless proved otherwise whereas the reverse is more likely to be true for women and minorities.

Some of the key points about stereotypes can be summarised as follows:

- They are, first of all, normal and necessary; they provide an initial basis for ordering the world and are an attempt to make sense of events around us.
- They can (and often do) however lead to incorrect evaluations of people.
- When we stereotype we essentially accept that within the group to which we belong (often referred to as the in-group) differences do exist between individuals; we also assume and accept that there are areas of similarity.
- When we observe or comment upon other groups (often referred to as the out-group) we tend to exaggerate the similarities of the members of that group and ignore the differences between them ('they're all the same anyway').
- Furthermore, we will also exaggerate the differences between different groups and minimise the similarities.
- Stereotypes can therefore create expectations based on group membership which can in turn lead to self-fulfilling prophecies.

One of the effects of stereotyping is therefore to deny individual uniqueness. A person is often responded to only as a member of a group instead of an individual with his or her own unique characteristics. This can then create difficulties in interpersonal communication and co-operation at work.

For example, Bettenhausen (1991) carried out one of the most comprehensive reviews of small-group research in which he examined the issue of groups with male and female members. Stereotyping and misattribution occurred consistently. Some of the findings included:

- The ability to recall contributions by group members was related to the speaker's sex, the female/male composition of the group and the subject.
- Female leaders' suggestions received more negative responses than the same suggestions put forward by a male leader.
- Men and women with high masculinity scores were perceived to have talked more and made better contributions.
- Men interrupted women more than other men and yielded to them less.

Trompenaars (1993), in his work looking at national cultural differences, provides a health warning by highlighting our (very human and natural) tendency to concentrate on the differences between people and to ignore the similarities. He identifies three dangers in doing this:

> First, a stereotype is a very limited view of the average behaviour in a certain environment. Second, people often equate something different with something wrong . . . Finally, stereotyping ignores the fact that individuals in the same culture behave according to the cultural norm. Individual personality mediates in each cultural system.
>
> (Trompenaars 1993: 27)

One implication of this could be that some of the differences between groups could be more *imagined* than real. This is obviously an area to address if different groups of people are to be assessed, developed and generally treated fairly within organisations. Falkenberg (1990) notes that stereotypes are resistant to change and yet little of the diversity literature has focused on improving the accuracy of stereotyping within work contexts.

Subtle and unrecognised cultural differences could also affect the way we view and interact with one another. Kennedy and Everest (1991), for example, think that some of the differences could relate to whether we come from high- or low-context cultures. People from high-context cultures usually see themselves as part of a group – often beginning with the family. In some cases, this has meant businesses reviewing the service they are offering to ensure they meet the needs of different markets. For example, in certain parts of the USA with large Hispanic populations McDonald's are building restaurants with larger seating areas because people from these communities tend to place a greater value on eating as a group.

Within the UK, work we carried out for a very large public-sector employer also revealed a very interesting difference in the way application forms were completed for that organisation's prestigious management training scheme. The forms asked for examples where individuals felt they had demonstrated the required competence. More than a third of the ethnic minority candidates gave examples that related to family life, whereas fewer than 10 per cent of the white candidates gave such examples. If the short-listers had put more weight on work-related activities then the minority candidates would have been relatively disadvantaged.

Flexibility is again the watchword here. Applying overrigid systems and processes could mean that real cultural differences will be ignored and as a consequence some people disadvantaged. It means being prepared to think through the reasons for deciding upon a particular policy, and to adjust and adapt them when necessary.

Reinforcing stereotypes: a danger of diversity

It should be noted that some of the work conducted in the name of diversity will enhance rather than reduce the effects of stereotypes, an issue touched on in Chapter 6. There is a real danger that by seeking to emphasise the differences between groups we ignore what is similar. Indeed, Kossek and Zonia (1993) suggest that this type of diversity training ie emphasising differences runs counter to the theories of reducing prejudices.

The new stereotypes being created are exemplified in numerous articles, particularly in the area of gender, where the supposed differences between men and women are highlighted. For example, Rigg and Sparrow (1994: 14) conclude that 'There is clear evidence of gender diversity in the style brought to jobs'. Their research, however, is based on a sample of only 12 male and four female middle managers.

There is much talk at the moment of managerial styles that encourage teamworking, development of staff etc. Some writers feel that this approach emphasises qualities women supposedly already possess, and therefore having more women in managerial positions will be a step towards this new style of management. For example, in a 1992 report by Proctor and Jackson about women in the National Health Service it is argued in the introductory text 'The culture of the health service defines a management task that is different . . . the management style most commonly associated with women is compatible with that culture' (p. 16). Furthermore, it continues, 'Tough management styles are incompatible with the NHS ethos and have eroded organisational commitment. It would seem that a people-oriented management style, more common among women than men, is more effective' (p. 16).

If this argument is accepted then the consequences must also be accepted. One of these is highlighted by Powell (1990: 72): 'Women are at risk when corporations assume that they have a monopoly on human resource skills. The risk is that they will be placed exclusively in managerial jobs that particularly call for special sensitivity and interpersonal skills . . . e.g. public relations, human resources management, consumer affairs, corporate social responsibility. These jobs are typically staff functions, peripheral to the more powerful line functions of finance, sales and production and seldom regarded in exalted terms by line personnel.'

The other consequence is that if people are prepared to accept the above assertion from the NHS about the relevance of women's skills they must also be prepared to accept a proposition along the following lines: 'In this organisation, we do not feel the people-oriented management style is appropriate. An objective, task-focused style, is what is required. As this style is more common amongst men than women it is likely that men will be more effective.' Such a statement, we believe, should rightly be greeted with a mixture of outrage and ridicule. And yet positive stereotypical statements about women are much more likely to be accepted uncritically.

Davidson (1991) suggests that numerous cross-cultural studies and reviews have concluded that there are far more similarities than differences between male and female managers, and that where differences do occur they are often related to:

- low proportions of female managers
- attitudinal differences caused by prejudice and discrimination
- different life circumstances and stresses of women managers in comparison with men.

Other research has also supported the conclusion of no real difference in male and female management, leadership or personality style (eg Ferrario 1991; Powell 1990; Bourantas and Papalexandris 1990; Bartram 1992). Powell (1990: 74) concludes that 'Organisations should not assume that male and female managers differ in personal qualities. They should also make sure that their policies, practices and programmes minimise the creation of sex differences in managers' experiences on the job'.

Stereotypes will also present problems to the management of diversity, as the tendency to treat people as members of groups, each sharing the same characteristics, runs counter to an approach based on individuals. Nevertheless stereotypes exist and the process represents a natural cognitive response. Managing diversity means attempting to break down stereotypes and make people aware of their dangers. Being educated on the cultural and gender differences that are perceived to exist, however, may not be the way to limit the effects of stereotyping – in fact they may serve to reinforce them. If in their diversity work people continue to emphasise the differences between groups and ignore areas of considerable overlap and similarity they will only serve to create more barriers.

Diversity competence

Faced with the need to deal with a diverse workforce and with the attendant myths and stereotypes that exist some authors have referred to the need for some additional skill or 'diversity competence'. For example, McEnrue (1993) describes the qualities needed for effective cross-cultural communication as:

- the capacity to accept the relativity of one's own knowledge and perceptions
- the capacity to be non-judgemental
- a tolerance for ambiguity
- the capacity to appreciate and communicate respect for other people's ways, backgrounds, values and beliefs
- the capacity to demonstrate empathy
- the capacity to be flexible
- a willingness to acquire new patterns of behaviour and belief
- the humility to acknowledge what one does not know.

Other required skills include those of managing change under circumstances where people are likely to have a variety of opinions about what should be done, or where too few resources exist to do what everyone wants. Others also refer to the necessity of being open-minded enough to learn to recognise and appreciate the differences (Dreyfuss 1990), of being prepared and able to understand the values and attitudes of others and of sensitivity to the stress of being in a minority (Kanter 1977). Kennedy and Everest (1991: 50) also agree that in order to manage diversity at an individual level we need to 'understand our own cultural filters and to accept differences in people so that each person is treated and valued as a unique individual'.

Yet the skills required are in the main interpersonal skills and those related to communication. These skills are described in other research without any reference to managing diversity. Argyris (1962) constructed a model that defined five conditions necessary for authentic relationships or interpersonal competence in organisations. These were:

- giving and receiving non-evaluative, descriptive feedback
- owning, and helping others to own, values, attitudes, ideas and feelings
- openness to new values, attitudes and feelings as well as helping others to develop their own degree of openness
- experimenting and helping others to do the same with new values, attitudes, ideas and feelings
- taking risks with new values, attitudes, ideas and feelings.

Stodgill (1974), having factor-analysed 52 studies on leadership, found that communication and interpersonal skills were mentioned more times in the literature than technical and administrative skills. Vaught and Abraham (1992) also show that there is considerable empirical research on personal communication and that effective communication has been linked with satisfaction, employee performance, lower work stress and leadership style.

This raises an interesting question: are the skills that recent authors are saying managers need today really so different from the skills that were always needed? The competencies managers require to manage a diverse workforce appear very similar to skills of communication competence that have been described for the last 30 years at least.

Some research appears to indicate that cultural differences within a group would lead to greater communication problems and other problems associated with the leadership role (Traindis, Hall and McEwen 1964; Anderson 1966). This merely underlines the central importance of communication to diversity management.

Other research reinforces the view that skilled managers should be capable of meeting the challenges a diverse workforce will bring. Anderson (1983) compared the performance of managers of ethnically homogeneous and heterogeneous groups: it was found that the effective leaders of the homogeneous groups displayed the same characteristics as the effective leaders of the heterogeneous groups. In both cases the leaders established effective strategies for tackling the tasks in hand. The role of the manager is to clarify the objectives and ensure that processes are developed to meet them effectively.

What can individuals do?

On a more individual level there are things that managers can do, including:

- *examining their own behaviour styles, beliefs and attitudes* – the sorts of attitudes to racial and cultural differences they may hold, and the sorts of stereotypes and assumptions they may have. It is important to bear in mind this refers not only to stereotypes of and assumptions made about ethnic minorities or women, but to all forms of bias which can enter into decision making.
- *considering their own feelings and reactions to people* – particularly if they find these individuals cause them irritation or annoyance. Trying to explore why they might cause that response. Trying to maintain a distance from events and explore them objectively. Is it a performance problem that is being dealt with or is it that the manager has difficulty accepting a different style of working? Is it that certain values that the manager or the organisation hold to be important are not being adhered to? If so, this needs to be discussed with the person concerned to see whether they agree. Masterson (1992: 50) makes the very useful and important distinction between disagreements and misunderstandings: 'Disagreements are by nature clear and explicit; they can be negotiated or acted upon. The difference with misunderstandings is that most of the time, we are not even aware they are taking place. Shared values can be hidden behind seemingly contradictory behaviours. One same behaviour can represent two very different value interpretations.'
- *being curious, getting to know their staff.* If there are people from different ethnic or cultural backgrounds, making opportunities to learn more about their backgrounds, about activities they may be involved in, their home life. More often than not people will welcome the opportunity to talk about the differences between their home life and their work life, rather than keep them completely separate.
- *trying to see things from other people's perspective.* If the

manager were in their shoes, how would he or she respond to the sorts of policies and procedures that the organisation is enacting? If the organisation is enforcing a particular style of dress or standard of conduct, how would people of different religions and backgrounds respond to it? We perceive the world through cultural filters and it is important to realise that the fact people from other communities and cultures may have different perspectives from our own on certain issues does not necessarily mean they are wrong.

- *being honest with staff.* If there are things that the manager finds confusing or perplexing about the way they are behaving then he or she should ask them about it. This is perhaps best illustrated with a quotation from the Lord Chancellor, Lord Mackay, addressing a conference on 'Race and Criminal Justice', when he said:

  > Opportunities for misunderstanding abound, even between people of goodwill whose sincerity is beyond question. Prejudice may exist and flourish, but be unrecognised as such. Then some incident, perhaps a chance incident, exposes it for what it is, or reveals what someone else perceives it to be. It is in this kind of way that we obviously fail to appreciate how others react to what we do or say. We are certain that we are not prejudiced. The danger is that we may be so confident we are not prejudiced that we do not appreciate the risk that something we say or do may reasonably be construed as pointing the other way.

- *examining their own communication style.* This may require more detailed and detached analysis, but to what extent are they open to new views, ideas, ways of working etc? How comfortable would they be in giving feedback to colleagues on their communication style and in receiving feedback on their own? Unless this degree of openness exists it will be difficult to create the circumstances under which effective management of diversity can take place.

- *looking at how flexibly they treat their staff* – trying not to expect everyone to conform to one particular style of working, as Buhler (1993: 19) says:

For years, managers were trained to treat everyone in their
employment exactly the same. In avoiding discrimination, sameness was stressed. Managers were taught that equality translated
into sameness. Today, however, mass changes are underfoot. To
treat employees fairly often means to treat them differently. Flexibility is the key in managing employees today: while the shift
toward flexibility has been seen in some areas, many managers
still rely on sameness in dealing with employees.

- *when leading teams, taking care that all people feel part of the
  team.* Managers should spend time with individuals and ensure
  that they feel valued – remember how easy it is to make people
  in minorities feel invisible! This can extend to issues that seem
  small but are very personal, like ensuring correct pronunciation
  and spelling of team members' names. They should be prepared
  to give and receive feedback and try to create an environment
  where different working styles can be accommodated.
- *working on developing their staff* – understanding what motivates them and what they want to obtain from work *at this
  moment in time*. It is important to recognise that people's motivation may, and invariably does, change over time and so it is
  important to check regularly whether their views on their role or
  the organisation have changed. Managers should look at the way
  they develop their staff and examine the extent to which they are
  giving all of their staff opportunities. Do some have obstacles to
  their development which, with a little flexibility and imagination
  on the manager's part, could be overcome? Managers should try
  to consider alternatives to traditional forms of development, for
  example mentoring or coaching. They should be prepared to del-
  egate tasks and give people the opportunity to experiment and
  take risks.
- *challenging accepted practices* – asking themselves whether the
  way the organisation currently does things is the best way. If an
  element of managing diversity means giving staff space to
  develop, it must also mean managers having the space to allow
  themselves to develop.
- *acting as a role model* – being aware of the fact that their behaviour will be seen as indicative of organisational priorities and

culture. By trying to value and develop all staff, by operating flexibly, by being open in communications, managers will be sending very positive messages to those around them.

Key points

- Being in a minority, of whatever kind, can lead to considerable difficulties, particularly in the way people in the majority view and evaluate performance. Research has shown tendencies to exaggerate poor performance of minorities and to ignore their contributions in meetings.
- Stereotyping, or generalised beliefs about groups of people, represents an obstacle to managing diversity. Often differences between groups may be more imagined than real. This means that organisations and individuals need to be more aware of what stereotyping is and how it can affect decisions.
- Diversity work, if it emphasises the differences between groups, could well lead to the reinforcement of stereotypes rather than contributing to their reduction.
- Several authors have recently attempted to define some form of diversity competence. However, their efforts have not resulted in anything radically different. Instead they reinforce the work carried out by, amongst others, Argyris approximately 30 years ago when he identified the importance at work of interpersonal skills and 'communication'. Other research has also shown that such competence is assessed as an important quality amongst successful managers and leaders. This is in fact another benefit of engaging in diversity work.
- Other research has also shown that managers who are good at managing so-called homogeneous teams possess the same qualities as those successful at managing so-called diverse teams. We would venture to suppose that such managers try to deal with people as individuals rather than expect everyone to be motivated by the same things, work in the same way and respond identically to any given stimulus. Good managers will also have a healthy degree of self-awareness and will be looking at ways to improve their own performance.

8

Gaining Diversity in Your Processes

This chapter examines the role of an organisation's processes in achieving, maintaining and developing diversity.

The processes an organisation has and the way they are operated are obviously critical ingredients in determining whether it is going to be successful in managing diversity. The processes to be examined here include:

- *recruitment*: attracting applicants, the organisation's image, methods of advertising
- *selection*: the methods used to select applicants, and ways of ensuring that the procedures are effective and fair
- *induction*: the process of socialising an individual into an organisation; these have been underresearched in the past but can have a tremendous impact on whether an individual stays with an organisation or not
- *appraisals*: the methods by which an individual's performance at work is assessed.

Recruitment

The complaint made by many organisations in that the main obstacle to achieving greater diversity in their workforce is that some sections of the population do not apply to them for work. For example, organisations which are male dominated will say that they get very few female applicants; others say that they get very few applications from ethnic minorities. It can be seen from the results of our own survey of 285 organisations (see Chapter 5) that the issues some of them will be addressing in the near future are to do with gaining greater diversity amongst applicants.

One solution to this is often to try to find ways of attracting those underrepresented groups specifically. This can include initiatives such as advertising in the ethnic press or advertising in publications more likely to be read by women. However, as has been identified in our own survey, positive action initiatives directed towards one specific group or another have tended not to be perceived as very successful. Again, the fundamental issue to be addressed is what is it about the organisation that fails to appeal to certain sections of the community? Having identified some responses to that particular question it is then possible to come up with some solutions.

Advertising in the ethnic press is a course many organisations take to attract ethnic minorities. Yet in our view it could be an example of jumping to a solution before the problem has been identified. Implicit in the action is the assumption that ethnic minorities do not read the national press, or that they believe the national press is bought only by white people. This is evidently not true. Ethnic minorities read the full range of daily newspapers in the same way that others in the population read them. In research we carried out for the Commission for Racial Equality (1989) we examined the extent to which organisations had implemented the CRE's Code of Practice. All of the case-study organisations had used the ethnic press at some point or another. However, it had worked for hardly any of them in that very few applications seemed to have been obtained through that route. And yet the organisations persisted in using the ethnic press, which puzzled us greatly. The logic appeared to be as follows:

> We get very few applications from ethnic minorities, therefore:
> - in order to address that issue we have advertised our jobs in the ethnic press;
> - we have however attracted few, if any, applications through this means from ethnic minorities;
> - we will nevertheless continue with this form of advertising even though it has not worked.

The persistent failure of the ethnic press for these organisations did not lead them to rethink their strategy. Merely advertising in the ethnic press may not be sending the message that the organisation wishes to convey. There may be more fundamental issues to do with the way an organisation or profession is perceived by those ethnic minorities that constitute a greater obstacle. Dealing with these issues can only be done by a more thorough analysis of the images projected in all areas of an organisation's activity including, for example, its marketing of products as well as its recruitment literature. The non-attractiveness of an organisation for particular groups is what is called in Northern Ireland the 'chill factor' ('a problem of attitude towards, and an environment within, the workplace. Members of a particular community can feel discouraged or prevented from applying for jobs in any company or undertaking perceived as being traditionally associated with the other community', Department of Economic Development 1989: 2). This needs to be addressed in the long term rather than with one or two short-term initiatives.

Diversity, it must be remembered, means more than just women, minorities and people with disabilities. The example in Table 8.1 illustrates how examining the more fundamental bases on which recruitment was conducted, rather than targeting a group specifically, led to more women being recruited.

Table 8.1
An example of development recruitment strategies
(Equal Opportunities Review 1993)

- BBC Engineering is male dominated, as one might expect. As eight out of ten engineering graduates are male, most of the applicants for engineering posts were male.
- In the 1980s the market for engineers became increasingly competitive and the BBC found that as competitors could offer better salaries it was starting to lose out.
- The Corporation decided to broaden its recruitment to include arts graduates and to offer people recruited in this way a specially tailored conversion training course.
- As 45 per cent of arts graduates are females, 'the BBC significantly increased its potential pool of female applicants'
- The BBC now consistently gets 30 per cent female applicants for its engineering places, despite the fact that the advertisements were not targeted at women.
- This example shows that reformulating your recruitment strategy and rethinking the foundations on which it is based can have beneficial results without targeting people according to their gender.

Selection

Having attracted a diverse group of applicants, the organisation must then see to it that the selection techniques are fair and effective.

It makes sense for any selection procedures to be as job-related as possible. This is crucial for a number of reasons, including legal ones. Under the provisions for indirect discrimination in the Sex Discrimination, Race Relations and Fair Employment Acts, organisations must show that their selection procedures are justifiable.

Under the Sex Discrimination Act (1975, 1986) Section (1)(1) (b) indirect discrimination is defined as the application of a requirement or condition to both men and women, more specifically one

   i) which is such that the proportion of women who can comply with it is considerably smaller than the proportion of men who can comply with it, and,
   ii) which he cannot show to be justifiable, irrespective of the sex of the person to whom it is applied, and
   iii) which is to her detriment because she cannot comply with it.

Similar provisions exist within the Race Relations Act and the Fair Employment Act. The more job-related selection procedures are, the greater the justification for using them will be.

The issues relating to indirect discrimination are still being explored in tribunals but the judgment made in the case of *Jones* v. *Chief Adjudication Officer [1990] IRLR 533 CA* provides some guidance in the development of selection procedures.

The 'demographic' argument is one way indirect discrimination can be established. Where one qualification is being challenged the process takes the following shape:

1. Identify the criteria for selection.
2. Identify the relevant population comprising all those who satisfy the other criteria for selection.
3. Divide the relevant population into groups representing those who satisfy the criteria and those who do not.
4. Predict statistically what proportion of each group should consist of women.

5. Ascertain what are the actual male/female balances in the two groups.
6. Compare the actual with the predicted balances.
7. If women are found to be underrepresented in the first group and overrepresented in the second, it is proved the criteria are discriminatory.

At this point it would then be up to the organisation to show that the procedures were in fact justifiable.

In the UK, if it was proven to be justifiable then the case would go no further. However in the USA, under the Civil Rights Acts of 1964 and 1991, an organisation could still be found guilty of discrimination if it was established that there were alternative techniques which would have had a less adverse impact on the groups and which an organisation refused to use. In this instance it is an obligation of the employer to ensure that they have looked at the alternative selection methods available and explored their viability. We believe that organisations should also follow that procedure here, just to make certain that the processes and procedures they are using are indeed the fairest and most appropriate for the jobs they are considering.

In developing selection procedures, therefore, organisations should look at techniques that provide a balance of validity (ie the effectiveness of the test or procedure) and fairness. In their review of selection techniques Pearn, Kandola and Mottram (1987) and Schmitt (1989) agree that to optimise efficiency and fairness the best techniques are:

- assessment centres ie 'an extended assessment procedure usually combining several techniques (tests, interviews, written exercises, group discussions) and several assessors who observe and rate a group of candidates' (Pearn *et al.* 1987: 86)
- work sample tests ie 'practical simulations of aspects of the job which have been carefully chosen, on the basis of systematic analysis, to represent key features of the job' (Pearn *et al.* 1987: 86).

Wood (1994) has recently reiterated the validity and fairness of work samples and predicts that their use will increase.

However, it should not be assumed that just because a technique in the research has been shown to be fair it will be fair in every application. Research carried out by Pearn Kandola and reported by Fullerton and Boyle (1994) shows for example how results of assessment centres are being accepted on the basis of blind faith rather than by assessing their fairness systematically. At the least, when operating selection processes organisations should be able to demonstrate the following:

- that a thorough job analysis has been conducted in order to establish the selection criteria. Wherever possible, the sample should have included a diverse group of people including for example women and ethnic minorities. If this is not possible then the criteria should be examined by someone knowledgeable about both selection and diversity issues.
- that the procedures to be developed map onto the competencies identified from the job analysis and that there is good point-to-point correspondence. The more closely the tasks to be performed in the selection process reflect the tasks to be carried out in the role, the fairer and more valid the procedure will be (Arvey and Faley 1988; Robertson and Kandola 1982).
- that processes have been piloted using diverse samples. Where discrepancies in performance occur these should be examined at this stage and if necessary repiloted. Feedback should be obtained from the sample about how they felt about the process. This could provide valuable information about how the procedures should be presented. Table 8.2 provides an example of this.
- that the people who will be involved in the selection process have been trained. This should include skills elements demonstrating how the process needs to be operated but also elements on improving objectivity and reducing bias.
- that monitoring of the processes takes place. At the least this should include gender and ethnic monitoring. If there are few members of ethnic minorities or women amongst the applicants then you should review your attraction methods to ensure that they are not indirectly discriminatory eg by the use of word-of-mouth recruitment.

- that the processes are reviewed on a regular basis and care is taken that the competencies you are using and consequently the processes themselves are still relevant.

Table 8.2

An example of how piloting and feedback can help develop fairer processes

- A series of work sample tests were developed for a major public-sector employer for entrants to a junior management position.
- One test was designed to test the competency of decision making.
- A test was devised requiring candidates to analyse written and numerical information and to make decisions within policy guidelines.
- The test, however, related to the purchase of different types of computers. After piloting the tests with people from the Department and external people, we found that many women said that they knew nothing about computers and so had not been able to answer the questions. Yet the test had been designed so that computer knowledge was not necessary. The resulting analysis showed that women did far worse than men.
- The test was redesigned and repiloted. The complexity of the information and amount of information remained unchanged. Rather than presenting information about computers it was on office furniture. This time a normal distribution of scores was obtained and the women did as well as the men.
- This experience highlighted to us the importance of presentation and format of the materials. By careful thought and design the procedures could tap into what they were designed to measure rather than the anxiety of candidates about factors irrelevant to the selection process.

An important issue related to selection procedures is the use of personality questionnaires. In his review of selection techniques Schmitt (1989) concludes that whereas personality instruments only revealed small differences between subgroups they had low validity. However, diversity may not be aided by the use of personality questionnaires to select clones. Personality test publishers and developers invariably advise organisations to use such instruments

only as one component of their selection process. In practice, however, our concern is that such practices do take place within organisations. Personality profiles will be developed for a job and then
each individual will have their profile matched against the organisational profile to look for a fit. Such a rigid application of profiles
could well limit diversity within teams. Table 8.3 provides an
example of an organisation applying all the above principles and
achieving:

- greater diversity
- savings in the selection process
- a high level of validity.

Table 8.3
An example of developing objective and
fair selection processes

- The Employment Service (a government agency) has over
  40,000 employees spread over a network of 1,600 local
  offices. Changes to the rules governing Civil Service recruitment meant the Employment Service could have much closer
  involvement in recruiting people to meet its specific business
  requirements.
- Demographic changes meant there would be fewer school-
  leavers entering the job market, but the Service saw this as an
  opportunity to attract recruits from other sections of the community. It also wanted to build teams of people that reflected
  the communities it served.
- The objectives of the project provided the essential foundation for all the subsequent work. These were:

  to recruit people with the skills and abilities to meet the
  needs of the business

  to be more cost-effective

  to develop fair selection procedures

  to have a devolved process

  to be flexible enough to adapt to local needs

  to promote a positive image of the Employment Service as
  an employer.
- A detailed competency analysis was undertaken by a team
  consisting of Employment Service and Pearn Kandola
  psychologists.

- Competencies were identified in draft form and given to focus groups to refine and revise.
- The agreed competencies formed the basis of *all* the subsequent recruitment and selection materials that were designed. These consisted of:

    a competency-based application form which asked applicants to produce evidence of skills and abilities directly related to competencies. It was accepted that such experience may have been acquired from any area of life – work, home, school etc. Little emphasis was placed on traditional selection criteria eg educational qualifications were not asked for. The form also communicated to applicants the competencies they would need to do the work.

    shortlisting guidelines with a systematic rating scheme developed to enable recruiters to be as objective as possible in dealing with the forms.

    work sample tests. The advantage of these was that they could be tailored to the competencies and continue the communication process to candidates as to what the job entailed and the competencies required.

    structured interview schedules, together with an interview rating form and decision guide. Again, this was done to ensure consistency and objectivity.

- All materials were piloted and trialled extensively before they were used.
- The results of a concurrent validation study of the tests produced a correlation coefficient of 0.61 – a gratifyingly positive outcome. Furthermore, analysis of the costs showed the process to be cheaper than the old system; it found a wider range of people (eg ethnic minorities and women) getting through the system.
- This example shows that it is possible, given a lot of care and some imagination, to achieve fair and effective selection processes.

Induction

One of the issues that emerged from research carried out by Gordon *et al.* (1991) and also identified by Cox (1991) is that people who are in minorities in organisations tend to take longer to be inducted and socialised. White males tend to take the least amount of time. This is perhaps understandable as there are more white male role models within most organisations and there are more people with whom they might feel comfortable and to whom they can turn for more information or support.

One thing that the Gordon research revealed was that women and ethnic minorities in particular were relatively unaware of the expectations placed on new employees and what they needed to do in order to make progress within the organisation.

Many employers offer what is known as a 'Cook's tour' of the organisation and this, for them, represents induction. Induction itself is a relatively underresearched area, although more attention is now being focused on it. The socialisation processes that take place early on in a person's career within an organisation can have an extremely long-lasting impact. Recent work by Bauer and Green (1994) has shown that the early impressions formed by newcomers can remain with them for many months. Similarly they found early involvement in work-related activities led to better integration into the organisation and greater productivity.

Although diversity was not specifically addressed it is easy to see how these results could be affecting minorities. If managers have made assumptions about the capabilities of newcomers based on stereotypes, or if they feel uncomfortable dealing with people from different groups, then this will have an adverse effect on minorities.

If an organisation's induction processes are not effective significant numbers of staff could leave relatively quickly and this could reflect on the validity of the selection processes. For example, if significant numbers of people leave the organisation it may be interpreted that the selection process has failed. However, it may be that the selection process was good and it was the induction process that failed.

Therefore, in order to improve their induction process organisations should:

- make it clear to individuals – all individuals – what the organisation values and what people need to do in order to make progress within it.

- have a mentoring process so that new people joining the organisation have access to experienced people who can give them advice and guidance where appropriate. Again, this will aid the socialisation of the person into the organisation. However, the people who act as mentors need to be carefully trained and be made aware of the importance of their role. Badly handled, mentoring can actually do more harm than good.
- ensure that the induction process is not so structured that individual concerns about the organisation, development etc cannot be handled.
- ensure that managers responsible for inducting new staff are properly trained, are aware that some people joining the organisation may experience more problems in settling down than others and are able to deal with this situation when it arises.

Appraisals

The appraisal process is critical for managing diversity within the organisation. Often an appraisal process will determine the language used to describe and evaluate performance within the organisation. It will also emphasise those types of behaviours which are considered to be important, those which are unimportant and indeed those which are not valued at all.

It is important that training and development are considered part of any appraisal process: if managers are unaware how to train and develop their staff they will be restricting the extent to which an organisation can fully tap into the potential of its employees. Furthermore, given that appraisals are often a one-to-one process they can offer considerable scope for bias. What can be done, therefore, to make the appraisal process fair to a diverse working population?

- First of all, the organisation needs to be sure the criteria by which people are being evaluated are relevant to the jobs they are carrying out and to the organisation as a whole. These are often described in the form of competencies, and the more behaviourally-based rather than personality-based they are the less chance there will be of subjectivity.

- Second, there needs to be a process for setting clear and measurable objectives for people within organisations. These are often referred to as SMART objectives ie Specific, Measurable, Achievable, Relevant and Timed. The importance of goal setting is well established within the psychological literature and has obviously influenced management thinking. Goals and objectives are far more likely to be achieved, and with a greater degree of satisfaction, if employees feel they have participated fully in establishing them. Merely giving people objectives can have the effect of reducing their motivation.

- Third, there needs to be an examination of the extent to which different ways of achieving those objectives are to be tolerated. Obviously there are certain core values that an organisation will have and it will expect people's behaviour to conform to these. Beyond that, though, being a diverse organisation means being able to respect the fact that not everybody works in exactly the same way and that there needs to be some tolerance of different working styles and patterns. If there is a restricted view taken not only of the setting of the objectives, but also of the means of achieving those objectives, then that will be an indication diversity is not being tolerated.

- Fourth, everyone needs to know what they should expect from the appraisal process and what they should do if these expectations are not being met. This includes managers being appraised as well as their staff. It means opening up the process to make it more of a dialogue rather than a handing down of instructions.

- Fifth, training needs to be given to managers in how to carry out the process. Many organisations in our experience fail on this point. They may well provide very good written information about the system but fail to back it up with adequate training. A good appraisal system will fail if it has untrained managers conducting it. This will soon lead to the system falling into disrepute and a degree of cynicism being generated about its operation.

- Sixth, potential must be examined further. Often this is very vaguely defined and can lead to highly subjective judgements being made. It is not uncommon in our experience to have men and women given equal ratings in current performance, and then to find that women will be rated lower in terms of their potential. Often it is very difficult to identify why this should be. One possible reason is that current performance is often very evidence-based, concrete and factual. Potential is far more subjective and is often based on a manager's interpretation of and extrapolation from current performance. As a consequence it is far more open to bias. A clear definition needs to be provided of what potential actually means and managers need to be instructed, informed and trained in how to interpret that part of the appraisal process.

- Seventh, the process needs to be audited regularly and quality checks carried out to ensure that managers are implementing the process to the required standards. Without such regular reviewing and updating standards could decline to the point that the appraisal process becomes relatively meaningless to everybody.

Table 8.4 provides an example of an organisation that audited its appraisal process to identify any potential biases within it against women and minorities. They discovered that the issues they needed to address were not limited to just those groups, but that they needed to see the process worked more effectively and fairly for everyone.

Table 8.4
Improving the appraisal process

- A certain public-sector organisation had recently changed its method of appraising staff.
- Previously it had been based on the assessment of personal qualities but now it was framed in terms of whether work objectives were being met, and performance was assessed within a competency framework.
- The organisation was concerned that there were few women or people from ethnic minorities in senior management and that this might be due to bias in the appraisal process.
- A thorough review was conducted of the process, including analysis of ratings, interviews and group discussions. We could find little in the way of overt bias against women and minorities.

- Instead the review showed that there were potential hazards to fairness, not just against women or minorities, but anyone.
- These included:
  - lack of standards in conducting the appraisal and completing the documentation. Some managers were obviously better than others.
  - lack of training in either the new or the old systems. Consequently many managers did not know what they were supposed to be doing anyway.
  - lack of openness about the system which led many people to perceive it as unfair. The way to improve the system and processes was by tackling these issues. It needed to work better for all staff, and to conform to standards set and constantly applied by well-informed, trained managers.

Jenkins (1986) outlined the concepts of the 'inclusive' and 'exclusive' approaches when examining racism and discrimination. These approaches can be applied to the recruitment, selection and career development processes that operate within an organisation. Table 8.5 details the characteristics of both these approaches.

Table 8.5
Characteristics of the exclusive and inclusive approaches

EXCLUSIVE	INCLUSIVE
A narrow and fixed view of the criteria and how they manifest themselves	An objective set of criteria, open to the various ways in which they manifest themselves
A focus on the 'type' of person who will be acceptable to the organisation and where they are likely to come from	Open to people of various types and backgrounds
Merit is insufficient	Merit alone is sufficient

Organisations that are effective in managing diversity base their processes on an inclusive approach. By doing so they ensure that the best candidates are selected, promoted and developed within the organisation. Essentially their human resource systems and processes (including promotion, career development and training provision) are not based on a rigid idea of the 'type' of person that would be viewed as acceptable by the organisation; rather, they are strongly focused on job-relevant criteria.

Key points

- Organisations need to ensure that their processes are as fair and objective as possible. If human resource processes are unfair and inefficient an organisation can achieve neither the objectives nor the benefits of being a diversity-oriented employer.
- This chapter has explored four key processes: recruitment, selection, induction and appraisal. Whilst there are obviously differences between them certain themes can be identified:
  - first, the need to ensure that any system clearly meets organisational requirements and that the criteria are job-relevant
  - second, the importance of creating the right organisational image, whether for employees or potential applicants – a key to this is openness in the procedures being operated
  - third, the need to make sure that managers are properly trained and that this training not only covers the skills and information needed to operate the system but also examines bias and how to reduce it
  - finally, the ever-present requirement to review and audit the processes to ensure they remain relevant and fair.

9

Positive Action and Targets: The Pieces That Do Not Fit

In this chapter targets, positive action and their relevance to a strategy on diversity are examined in more detail. There has been much debate on the effectiveness of positive, or affirmative, action measures in the USA. Some feel that such actions are unnecessary, even unhelpful. Others suggest that if such measures are not taken issues relating to equality, particularly those relating to sexism and racism, will be neglected.

Our view is that an approach whose underpinning philosophy is the needs of the individual will automatically be compromised when any actions are based purely on someone's supposed group membership. The recent debates on these issues are presented here together with research that has attempted to examine the psychological impact of affirmative action.

Background to the debate

As can be seen from our own research data (see Chapter 5) one of the key differences between the most and least successful initiatives was the issue of *universal benefit*. With positive action initiatives, however, the perceived beneficiaries will have been chosen primarily on the grounds of their race or gender. To many people this goes against the idea of fairness to everyone regardless of any other factors such as race, sex, disability and nationality.

The argument often put forward in support of positive action is that it helps those who are disadvantaged get to the 'starting-line', or that it helps create a 'level playing-field' for disadvantaged groups by enabling them to compete effectively with others in the organisation. This type of approach forms an important ingredient of many equal opportunities strategies but needs to be fundamentally reconsidered as part of a managing diversity approach. If managing diversity truly is about creating an environment where everyone feels valued and their talents are being fully utilised, then *actions ought to be targeted on any individual who has a particular developmental need and not restricted to individuals who are members of particular groups* (see the example in Table 9.1).

Table 9.1
An example of addressing individual needs rather than group membership

A transport organisation was selecting staff for specialist and important positions. To do this they operated a procedure that involved interviews, psychometric tests and practical tests.

Most of the candidates were internal and there were significant numbers of ethnic minorities who applied. None of the ethnic minority applicants was successful. It appeared that the aptitude tests in particular presented a very considerable barrier. The organisation decided to investigate this further and we were called in to assist them.

A session was arranged with some of the unsuccessful applicants where we asked them how they felt about taking the tests. Many of them had not taken such tests before and felt stressed beforehand. These feelings were not alleviated by the apparent coldness of the proceedings.

We asked them to take some tests while we observed them. We soon discovered that their test-taking strategies were not very good. For example:

– Some did not monitor how they were progressing against the clock.
– Others would continue working through the items in order even though they would have done far better to have skipped difficult items and returned to them later.
– Many were confused by the instruction 'to work quickly and accurately without wild guessing'. They invariably chose to work accurately at the expense of speed.

It was clear that lack of test sophistication was handicapping their performance. To help overcome this an open learning booklet on test-taking skills was developed. Trialling of the booklet showed that by improving test-taking strategies test performance could be improved. So far, so good. The problem arose at the next stage. The organisation was approached by an equal opportunities group who maintained that this booklet should only be available to women as they were underrepresented in that particular type of work. However, another lobby felt that it should be made available only to ethnic minorities as they too were underrepresented. In truth, the booklet would not have been distributed on gender grounds, as black men would have had access to it; nor would it have been distributed on ethnic grounds as white women would have had access to it. It would have been easier to say that if you were a white male applicant, you could not have it!

Our advice was that this booklet should be made available to all candidates – the ones who would benefit the most would be those who lacked test-taking knowledge. It was the *need* that had to be addressed rather than *group membership*.

Different views of affirmative action

Burstein (1992) considers that there are competing views of affirmative action:

- a 'remedial action' view ie such policies are needed to counteract the effects of past discrimination
- a 'delicate balance' view ie helping minorities without adopting actions that harm the majority
- a 'no preferential treatment' view ie individuals should not be given preference based on group membership.

The 'remedial action' view held sway from the 1960s to the mid-1980s, but since then there has been increasing support for the 'no preferential treatment' view.

Nevertheless this approach to equal opportunities is not necessarily welcome. For example, Dickson (1992: 46) asserted: 'In capitalism's focus on profit and competition, I have found and expanded a professional foothold for people of color.' He goes on to state that he believes 'in the business model of making a better world for minorities', and furthermore that:

Quite simply, business needs the best and the brightest, regardless of race and ethnic background and to meet that need, corporate America is willing to make a place for diversity . . . beyond anything we've ever seen before. There are great problems to be overcome, of course, including a lot of lingering prejudice. There is also a condition – namely that minority members must be able to give

business what it needs, both in skills and in behaviour. But, the fact
remains that US corporate leaders want to recruit young people of
color and *want* them to shatter the glass ceiling and rise to their
levels of greatest competence.   (Dickson 1992: 46)

This article provoked a thoughtful and interesting response from
many people seen as important in the managing diversity arena.
Some felt that affirmative action may not represent a wholly positive way forward. For example, Drake (1992: 142) states that: 'If a
corporation is committed to working objectively to hire the best
and brightest in a diverse culture, many inequalities will take care
of themselves.' He goes on to say that: 'Unfortunately, over time,
the application of affirmative action has been misused and the term
itself today has negative connotations.'

Drake was supported in this view by Mason (1992: 146), who
says:

> Every individual deserves the right to succeed or fail based on per-
> formance. That requires management and peer support and accept-
> ance, opportunity, challenge, mentoring and honest feedback. None
> of these needs is any way different from what a white male needs to
> achieve, with one exception: a concerted effort to eliminate devaluing
> of individuals based on superficial differences, namely race.

Some writers (eg Pena 1992; Thompkins 1992) feel that limited
forms of affirmative action are probably necessary. Pena (1992:
149) says: 'Sometimes affirmative action programmes are the only
way to get minorities through the door. After that, the employee
must demonstrate his or her own capabilities for success.'

Others are sceptical about reducing the central importance of
affirmative action. One concern is that race issues would be ignored
if there was a move to more 'homogenised' diversity programmes.
Jones (1992: 156) says that: 'If this continues, diversity could
become the basis to eliminate corporate racial progress.' This view
has also been taken up by others, for example Thomas and Evans
(1992). However, this reflects the fact that some people see the
issues of diversity affect their primary area of interest and concern,
in this instance race.

Research on the effects of affirmative action and the 'stigma of incompetence'

Much of what is written on positive or affirmative action is based purely on conjecture, opinion and anecdotal evidence. It also takes, as you might expect, a very quantitative approach to the issue, with success being measured by the numbers of different types of people employed. Very little writing has been based on scientific research which seeks to explore the impact of such action not just in numbers but also in terms of psychology.

One recently published paper (Heilman 1994) not only provides an extensive review of the relevant literature but also contains several carefully designed research studies. Her conclusion is that in situations where a person feels they have been selected for reasons other than their competence there will be a knock-on effect in terms of their self-confidence, and that this could lead to feelings of inadequacy: 'preferential selection may be interpreted as an indication that the recipient is not competent enough to be selected on his/her own merits' (Heilman 1994: 129). Another important finding from her own research and reviews of the literature is that if there is a feeling preferential selection is being operated then all groups are more likely to consider the selection processes unfair.

Furthermore, those who are selected in situations where preferential selection appears to be operating experience more stress than people selected by merit. This statistically significant finding is consistent with models of organisational stress 'which suggest that strain reactions develop as a consequence of the perceived inability to deal with job demands' (Heilman 1994: 141).

Other research has also shown that people perceived to have been selected by preferential selection are viewed more negatively by others in the organisation, including those of the same sex. Furthermore, when organisations make overt and explicit references to affirmative action unfavourable evaluations are made of the qualifications of minorities who are selected. Heilman (1994: 142) calls this 'the stigma of incompetence' and says the fact that it 'taints the recipients of the benefits of affirmative action is yet another unintended consequence of this policy'.

She seeks to explain why this might be the case by reference to Kelley's discounting principle (Kelley 1972; Kelley and Michela 1980). This says in effect that if someone is perceived to have been selected through affirmative action measures this will provide observers with a likely reason why the person was taken on, and the role of the individual's qualifications will be discounted. This leads to another assumption, namely that the individual is not as competent as others because if they were they would have been selected without the assistance of affirmative action. Relationships are affected because the beneficiaries of affirmative action are continually confronted with ambiguous situations. If they receive praise this may be seen as not genuine and if they receive criticism it is due to the antagonism of the group to which they belong.

A distinction is made between different types of affirmative action, and these can be described along a continuum from 'hard' to 'soft'. At the soft end are essentially merit-based procedures, although they still have the aim of trying to increase the numbers of applicants from particular groups, for example. At the hard end are the more quota-type approaches. The closer to the hard end the affirmative action was considered to be, the more negative was the perception of the individual's competence. 'In short, all of the consequences we have identified to result from affirmative action are likely to be worsened when merit criteria are thought to be of little importance in decision making' (Heilman 1994). (It is perhaps no surprise therefore to find that actions taken at the hard end of the spectrum, particularly targets, were amongst the least successful actions in our survey.)

There are inevitably consequences for those who would not appear to benefit from affirmative action, and these are primarily white males. To speak out against such measures could be interpreted as indicating residual suppressed prejudice. As Lynch and Beer (1990: 67) point out, 'it is inappropriate to attribute to old-fashioned prejudice all of whites' unhappiness with affirmative action. Positive views about such actions will be undermined if they perceive that the beneficiaries are not particularly competent. The effect will show itself in reduced motivation and commitment.'

Heilman's conclusions are, not suprisingly, critical of what affirmative action can achieve: 'Our research suggests that, as currently construed, affirmative action policies can thwart rather than promote workplace equality. The stigma associated with affirmative action can fuel rather than debunk stereotypical thinking and prejudiced attitudes' (Heilman 1994: 164). Finally, she states that:

> Providing women access to jobs traditionally reserved for men in our society does not necessarily further their cause. Access does not signify acceptance and access most certainly does not guarantee advancement. In fact, as long as affirmative action is associated with an absence of quality standards, it seems as likely to stimulate problems for women in work settings as it is to remedy them. The hidden costs of affirmative action can be very expensive indeed.
>
> (Heilman 1994: 164)

This theme is picked up by Small (1991) in an article comparing racial parity in the USA and England. It is subtitled 'We got to go where the greener grass grows!', referring to the fact that surveys in both countries reveal that people in the one believe the racial equality situation is better in the other. Having examined the research he concludes that affirmative action is 'both a smoke-screen and shield; the former because it diverts attention away from more fundamental aspects of equality, causes whites to fight with blacks and blacks to fight with each other over a reformist measure; the latter because it provides an acceptable issue for those who harbour more serious racial animosity to have a vent for their hatred' (Small 1991: 21). He is not entirely dismissive of affirmative action but does think that 'We must remain aware of its limitations and not direct too much energy in that direction so as to exhaust energies for other battles' (Small 1991: 22)

The implications for positive action in the UK

We believe that the above discussion has important implications for the shape and direction of positive action initiatives in the UK, especially so if the theme of diversity is to be picked up and effectively implemented rather than be used as an empty slogan or, worse, merely as an alternative phrase for equal opportunities.

Many organisations provide, for example, what is known as personal effectiveness or assertiveness training for women. In a recent UK survey produced by the Local Government Management Board (1993) 61 per cent of local authorities had provided assertiveness training for women; this seems to be an astonishingly high figure, and one cannot help thinking there is an element of keeping up with the Joneses with this type of exercise. Evidently it will have been seen that this particular group – women – has a need for such training. If one was to provide a definition of the issue, it would go along the lines that 'lack of assertiveness is a problem for women'. As the problem has been defined in this way, the solution obviously has to be applied to women. (Incidentally, Powell (1990), in a review of the literature, concludes that there are few differences between women and men in terms of workstyle. He states that: 'Women managers do not need to be sent off by themselves for "assertiveness training": they already know how to be assertive. Instead, they need access to advanced training and development activities such as executive MBAs or executive leadership workshops, just like male managers do' (Powell 1990: 73).)

However, an alternative way of viewing this would be to say that 'lack of assertiveness is a problem'. The solution to this problem would then be to provide assertiveness training to anybody felt to be lacking in this area, *regardless of their sex or ethnicity*. Provision would be based on an individual's need for development, rather than their group membership. This could be seen as a managing diversity response to the particular issue, as it

- focuses on the individual rather than the group
- addresses an organisational objective as well as an individual one
- seeks to include everyone in the process
- tries to ensure that everyone can make their maximum contribution to the organisation and achieve their fullest potential.

The conventional approach to positive or affirmative action means that whereas some people are benefiting by virtue of their group membership, others are excluded even though their developmental need may be as great, if not greater. As Powell (1990: 73) concludes, 'Women and men should be recommended for training and development according to their individual needs rather than their sex'.

This can be further illustrated by the failure of positive action training for ethnic minorities undertaken by the Trustee Savings Bank (TSB) (Cannon 1993). Pre-recruitment training was set up in a London college by the TSB in order to attract more ethnic minorities into the bank. The course was open only to ethnic minorities. The philosophy underlying this approach could be summed up as follows:

> ethnic minorities are not joining the bank;
> – therefore they must be lacking the basic skills required to enter the bank;
> – consequently, ethnic minorities, and they alone, must be given additional training to enable them to join the bank.

According to Cannon the initiative had some early success, particularly as a recruitment and public relations exercise, but there were complications later when some of the students were employed by the bank. The turnover of people who had attended the positive action pre-recruitment training was higher than for staff generally. A review discovered that some of the problems related to the candidates' lack of basic skills required by the bank. As Cannon states, 'insufficient assessment was made by the bank as to whether or not candidates met, or nearly met, the selection criteria' (Cannon 1993: 28). This led to problems when they were employed within the bank and, as a consequence, they were less likely to survive their probationary period.

Other problems were caused by lack of line management ownership: branch managers viewed the initiative with some suspicion and had little understanding of what the objectives of the course were. Nor were clear objectives set to define why this initiative was important. The result clearly bears out the findings of the Heilman research.

The solution to this has been to take a more holistic organisational approach which includes strategies such as:

- addressing why ethnic minorities with the relevant skills did not apply to them in the first place
- examining the organisation's advertising
- developing links with community groups
- examining selection methods
- training interviewers
- gaining commitment from the top of the organisation.

As Cannon (1993: 31) states, 'it is vital that a package approach is taken and the initiative forms part of a wider strategy on equal opportunities'.

Positive action, in our view, is no better than applying a sticking-plaster to a festering wound: it addresses the symptoms rather than the causes. It also provides activity without being purposeful. In many instances the reasons why an organisation fails to recruit women and minorities will be to do with the culture of the organisation and the image it projects. When faced with similar issues to those at the bank, organisations need to return to the fundamental premises of managing diversity, namely:

- why does the organisation fail to attract *suitably qualified* minority applicants in the first place?
- how fair and effective are the processes that are operated?
- how skilled are the managers in operating those processes?
- how committed are the managers to creating and maintaining a diverse organisation?

The TSB is not the only organisation that has carried out such initiatives, but they are one of the few who have openly reported the results. They are to be commended for their honesty as it provides other organisations with an opportunity to learn from their experiences.

An alternative approach is provided by Sainsbury's. They launched a scheme called 'Choices' for weekly-paid staff that aims to give them greater career choices through career guidance sessions. The second stage of the scheme, called 'Help Yourself to Education', involves sponsoring staff to gain further qualifications through studying in their own time.

The Director of Corporate Personnel at Sainsbury's, Judith Evans, is quoted as saying 'we recognised there were a number of people in the weekly-paid section, who probably had the talent to do more. If we could get more people moving forward, it would save us having to recruit as many trainee managers and hopefully reduce turnover amongst the weekly paid' (Donaldson 1993: 13).

It can be inferred from this that:

- Sainsbury's wished to explore the talent that was available in a large section of their workforce, namely the weekly paid.
- Their concern was to identify *individuals* who had untapped potential regardless of their race or gender.
- By targeting this level it would proportionately assist more women than men, because 70 per cent of weekly-paid staff are female. But the scheme could not be criticised for not providing equality of opportunity because *all people* in the weekly-paid bands were eligible to join it regardless of sex or ethnicity.

This appears to us to epitomise the diversity-oriented approach to developing the workforce because:

- It identifies the blockages that obviously exist for certain groups within the organisation.
- It is the blockage that is addressed, not the group: an attempt is made to remove the blockage so that the systems work better for all and not just one group.
- It attempts to address underlying issues rather than just the symptoms.
- As a consequence it is something that needs a long-term commitment rather than relying on short-term initiatives.
- It has an organisational goal as well.

The implications for targets

As can be seen from our own research (Chapter 5) targets are the least successful of the initiatives undertaken. It is difficult to draw any firm conclusions from the survey alone about why this may be, but it is possible to form some hypotheses based on our own experience of dealing with organisations.

In our experience, perhaps the most fundamental error organisations have made in setting targets is that they are often unrealistic. Saying that you want all parts of your workforce to be representative of the local community may sound fine and appear very laudable but may be very difficult to achieve in practice. For example, one London local authority for whom we worked had stated that all parts of the organisation, in terms of both level and department, should reflect the local community. This meant that there had to be a 15 per cent representation of ethnic minorities in all departments and at all levels. This presented a very difficult problem for, amongst others, the Architects Department. It was estimated that, of students at architecture schools, far fewer than 15 per cent were from ethnic minorities. If they were to achieve the target, then it would have to mean *overrecruiting* from ethnic minorities studying architecture.

The first thing to be done in order to set targets, therefore, is to make a realistic assessment of the relevant labour market.

The second mistake often made is that movements within the organisation (eg by promotions, transfers, secondments, people leaving or joining the organisation etc) are not properly calculated in order to provide a realistic idea of opportunities available in the near future. The example in Table 9.2 illustrates the point.

Table 9.2
An example of poor target setting

The client is a large, internationally renowned organisation with a London-based headquarters and several regional bases. It has made a strong commitment to equal opportunities and has taken many initiatives over a period of years.

In 1991 it announced that targets were to be established for women, ethnic minorities and people with disabilities.

The regions were asked to produce draft targets for their own offices on the basis that they were more familiar with their staff and with the make-up of the local workforce.

Some of the regions were surprised to find that the targets they were given by headquarters were significantly higher than their recommended figures. No negotiation of these targets was countenanced despite the efforts of some of the personnel managers within the regions.

One region approached us and asked whether the set targets were achievable within the time-scales. Human resource planning figures were given to us for the previous year (1990). These figures showed age profiles, gender distribution, ethnic distribution, promotions, resignations, new staff appointed etc.

As might be expected, none of the management team was female. In addition, they were also relatively young. At the level below that there was one woman, several more at the level below that, and more as one went further down through the grades.

In order to create some space at the top of the organisation, we worked on the assumption that the oldest member of the management team might take early retirement. His place on the management team would have to be taken by the woman at the grade below. In turn her place would also have to be taken by a female and we continued this process throughout the grades.

Working on this basis, which assumes that only the women would be taking advantage of the job opportunities that arose, the target was still not achievable.

Furthermore, although this meant that progress was made towards the gender target very little progress would be made towards the target for ethnic minorities!

Since the early 1990s of course very little recruitment has been taking place – indeed this organisation, like many others, has been de-layering and reducing costs. Consequently, the circumstances that existed when the targets were set no longer apply. Ideally the targets ought to be reviewed and readjusted. However, the public commitment to them has meant that any changes to them would almost certainly attract negative attention and so this has not been done, even though it is known that they are not achievable by legal means.

The second thing to be done when setting targets therefore is to take into account the opportunities that are going to become available in the near future and, by using the existing workforce profile, make a projection of the forecast position.

The difference between a forecast or a projection and a target is that a projection is much more flexible and takes into account all manner of considerations which may not have been apparent when the calculations were first made. As a consequence it is far more sensitive to the particular pressures the organisation may be experiencing at any moment.

Targets, on the other hand, give the impression of being (and often are) fixed and inflexible. Once established and communicated they are difficult to draw back from. While the mere setting of them may initially give the appearance of progress, if they have been inappropriately set and are unrealistic they will ultimately leave a feeling of failure. Furthermore, while some people in the organisation may well feel very positive about the targets set, others, particularly those who see their prospects as having been diminished, will view them rather more negatively. For example, if an organisation says that it wishes to increase the number of women at senior management levels to 40 per cent over the next two years and there are at the moment considerably fewer than that in senior management positions, it could appear to many men that they are being relatively disadvantaged in order for the target to be achieved, and that the priority is to get women, and not necessarily the best people, into management. This will naturally cause resentment and with resentment will come resistance. The wider cause of equality and fairness will have been subjugated to the desire to see the specific targeted groups advance through the organisation. An example of that is provided in Table 9.3.

The third mistake made when setting targets is the failure to have adequate feedback mechanisms. Managers could well be told the targets but may have had little or no input when they were established. Being told what to do in this fashion is no way to generate commitment to these issues. This is further compounded in many organisations by lack of feedback and consultation on progress towards the target. Managers can then feel they are being blamed for lack of achievement without necessarily having been asked their opinion why any failure occurred.

The example in Table 9.2 highlights this point. Here an attempt was made to involve managers in setting the targets, but their input

Table 9.3

An example showing tensions of a group-centred approach to recruitment

A certain engineering-based organisation wished to recruit more women as engineers. Over a period of years the organisation had promoted a positive image of itself as one where women had a future. For example a booklet focusing specifically on women had been published for female undergraduates. Graduate recruiters had also been made aware of the need to ensure women were treated fairly.

The result of this was that by the early 1990s approximately 40 per cent of the engineering graduates taken on were female. We were asked to undertake a review of the graduate recruitment process. We found that:

– there was a lot of subjectivity in the process. It was virtually impossible to tell for example why some people had been rejected or selected. There was a structured process for the interviews but interviewers were not following it.

– although the proportion of women selected compared to those who had applied was high, the opposite was true for ethnic minorities. Many minority candidates were treated dismissively.

The focus on women had led recruiters to examine their treatment of that particular group, which is no bad thing in itself. However, no attempt had been made to review or revise the selection process to make it fairer. It still appeared to be subjective and biased but, as it now favoured women, there was little or no complaint. The group-focused approach also meant that those groups not at the centre of the organisation's attention got short shrift. Finally, and more seriously, the fact that it was difficult to tell why people had been selected meant that it was unlikely this was an efficient approach to selecting future managers.

was then effectively sidelined. The result of such actions will be lack of commitment to the objectives and cynicism about the actual intentions (ie they are designed less to ensure people are treated fairly than to have the numbers turn out right).

The third thing to be done therefore when establishing the projections is to involve managers in the process. Once they are established there must be periodic reviews and feedback to the managers and staff.

Table 9.4

An example of two organisations' approaches to establishing greater ethnic and gender diversity

We are grateful to Robert Hayles, Vice-President for Diversity in Pillsbury Foods in the USA, who provided us with this example.

Organisation A decided to establish clear and challenging targets for these two categories of people. These were published and communicated to managers, who were told that they had to be met and that if they were not their bonus would be negatively affected.

Organisation B, no less committed to diversity, decided to adopt another route. Managers were told that the organisation would be reviewing the way it assessed, developed, promoted and generally treated its staff to ensure that it was making the best use of the potential available to it. A diversity education and training series was also initiated. Some people within the organisation felt that this approach was not sufficiently goal-driven, but they persisted with it.

The results within the two organisations were very interesting.

Organisation A achieved its objectives within their allotted time span. However in the following years the numbers of minorities and women actually fell. The organisation had been successful in recruiting minorities but its culture had not changed and remained uninviting to anyone who did not fit in with corporate norms.

In organisation B the numbers of women and minorities employed gradually increased but lagged behind those in organisation A in the early years.

However, the numbers of women and minorities continued to increase even as they began to decline in organisation A and surpassed it within three years.

The key differences in terms of approach, were that:

- Organisation B articulated a vision that was inclusive and the link could be made directly to business goals; organisation A articulated a vision that was exclusive – it applied to women and minorities only – and there was no direct link with business goals.
- Organisation B involved people in achieving their vision; organisation A adopted a command-and-control approach to achieving their goals.
- Organisation B took a long-term approach and was trying to achieve lasting cultural change; organisation A took a short-term approach and was primarily concerned with achieving numerical goals without giving sufficient consideration to the organisational culture issues which needed to be addressed if real, sustainable progress was to be made.

There are two reasons for doing this. First it enables people to understand the progress that is being made, and second it enables any problems to be identified, acknowledged and addressed. (Alternative approaches to forecasting and projection are presented in Table 9.4.)

In both these cases it can be seen that first of all the rationale for taking action is not to improve or change the numbers but *to improve the quality of human resource systems and management skills that exist within the organisation.* Second, the examples show that while organisations cannot guarantee they will achieve specified numbers, all other things being equal, there should be a change in the numbers over a period of time. This represents a form of benchmarking rather than absolute target setting.

Targets are therefore problematic not only in the ways they are currently established but also in the basic philosophy behind them. Singling out people for attention because of one particular factor (eg their colour or gender) will invariably mean, whether this is the intention or not, that members of those groups will receive special attention. This may be all well and good if you are a member of those targeted groups, but extremely unfortunate if you are not.

The other fundamental problem with targets is that they avoid active consideration of the processes organisations use to make decisions about people and the skills of the managers in using those processes. As long as the numbers turn out right the presumption will be that everything is fine. As Thomas (1990: 308) points out:

> Efforts often centre on numerical targets as indicators of progress. The governing assumption appeared to be they [the minorities, women] would assimilate. Historically, the affirmative action option has not called for permanent organisational changes. The adjustment burden has been on these individuals.

Our view is that unless you have confidence in both your systems and your managers this is a very big assumption to make. Of course, if you did have confidence in those two aspects then you would not need targets anyway!

Small (1991: 19) also notes another side-effect of targeting, namely tokenism:

The limited representation of blacks in business, in the professions and in academia has given rise to a widespread incidence of tokenism. This led to an assumption on the part of many institutions that once they had got an acceptable number of black recruits – usually in single figures – they need look no further.

The same issue, he believes, also exists for women.

Woo (1990) also highlights the dangers of such processes when a minority group has the audacity to fulfil its potential. She provides numerous examples from the early decades of this century when admission policies in some US universities were altered to prevent so many Jews from enrolling. As she notes, 'affirmative action, therefore, truly began decades ago on behalf of white Gentile males, long before programmes were initiated on behalf of disadvantaged minorities' (Woo 1990: 29). This issue has now re-emerged but this time it is Asian Americans who are viewed as the overrepresented group (or, as she provocatively puts it, 'the yellow peril'). She gives examples of university presidents who feel that in the interests of 'diversity' the number of such people entering university needs to be controlled.

Targets and positive action also have the effect of raising the importance of a person's ethnicity, colour or gender. If that person then fails to make the grade there is an increased likelihood that 'the inference may be made that race or sex is responsible for that failure' (Crosby and Clayton 1990).

Key points

- There is a debate currently in the USA about the merits of positive, or affirmative, action. The 'remedial action' view, prevalent from the 1960s to the mid-1980s, is now giving way to a 'no preferential treatment view'.
- Research on affirmative action has led Heilman (1994) to conclude that such action does not even help the targets – they become labelled with what she refers to as the 'stigma of incompetence'.
- The debate has implications for positive action within the UK. By targeting specific groups for action, organisations are implicitly saying that the groups themselves are part of the

problem for their lack of progress. For example, by giving assertiveness training only to women, a commonly taken initiative, it suggests that the women are the problem.

- The example from the Trustee Savings Bank highlighted how taking positive action can not only lead to problems once staff are employed but also distracts attention from the real organisational culture issues that need to be addressed.
- Similarly, targets are a potential problem within a diversity-oriented organisation in that they focus attention on the numbers of people employed from different groups rather than the quality of the processes used in selecting them.
- Organisations need to consider alternatives to targets such as benchmarking or workforce projections based on a realistic assessment of the current situation, together with an informed view of the future. Too often targets set are unrealistic and unachievable, but will give the impression of progress.
- Overall, because of their emphasis on groups rather than individuals, targets and positive action are the pieces that do not fit easily within the diversity mosaic.

10

MOSAIC: Our Vision of the Diversity-Oriented Organisation

Throughout the previous chapters the need to change the way organisations are currently structured and managed has been made explicit. Thus far, however, no vision of what this 'organisation of the future' would look like has been formulated. Filling this gap is the aim of the present chapter.

A change in tone and direction is required. We will be moving away from examining concrete data and presenting definitive assessments towards hypothesising about the characteristics we view as making up the diversity-oriented organisation.

Other writers on diversity have presented their view of what this organisation would look like (Cox and Blake 1991; Hall and Parker 1993; Gordon *et al.* 1991). The views of these writers will be outlined in presenting our own vision of the characteristics of the diversity-oriented organisation. The link with the concept of the learning organisation will also be examined.

Steps on the way

As outlined in Chapter 6 managing diversity must pervade the entire organisation if it is to be effective: it must be an organisational strategy. It follows that the diversity-oriented organisation will not be realised over a short period of time, rather it should be developed via a long-term change programme.

The possible stages an organisation would go through on its journey towards managing diversity have been outlined by both Thomas (1991) and Cox (1991). Thomas has developed a three-step evolutionary model.

The first step involves affirmative action, the primary purpose being to attain diversity within the organisation. Such policies, though, can leave the organisation's culture untouched. If individuals appointed as the result of an affirmative action programme fail it will be assumed that the individuals are somehow deficient.

The second step is to value diversity ie to gain an appreciation and understanding of how different groups of people in the workplace may differ from one another. However, valuing diversity in and of itself is insufficient in a diversity-oriented organisation, an opinion held very strongly by Thomas (1994: 324): 'You can accept, understand, and appreciate differences, even be free of racism and sexism, and still not know how to manage diversity.'

The third step is to manage diversity, and it is at this point that the potential of individuals is released. Managing diversity approaches seek to address issues related to core culture, values and ways of operating. In essence, the diversity-oriented organisation has evolved.

Cox (1991) presents a different categorisation. In his view organisations can be classified into one of three types: monolithic, plural and multicultural. In the monolithic organisation one majority group predominates, traditionally the white male group. There will be a small representation of women and ethnic minorities but they will be found mainly in the lower levels of the organisation. Minority groups entering the organisation will be expected to adapt to the existing norms and culture – one which places little importance on the integration of minority groups and which tolerates discrimination and prejudice.

However, Cox believes that the monolithic organisation is now a rarity and has been surpassed by the evolution of the plural organisation. The plural organisation is more inclusive of minority groups, although this representation is still predominantly in non-managerial roles. The driving force behind this integration is a strategy of affirmative action, an approach which ultimately leads to greater inter-group conflict. While discrimination and prejudice are reduced in the plural organisation, minority groups are still expected to assimilate into the majority culture. The majority of organisations in the 1990s are thought to fall into this category.

The multicultural organisation is Cox's vision of the diversity-oriented organisation. In his view it is one where people from non-traditional backgrounds can contribute and achieve to their fullest potential. The multicultural organisation will have six specific features:

- pluralism ie reciprocal acculturation, where all cultural groups respect, value and learn from one another
- full structural integration of all cultural groups so that they are well represented at all levels of the organisation
- integration of minority culture group members into the informal networks of the organisation
- an absence of prejudice and discrimination
- equal identification of minority and majority group members with the goals of the organisation and with opportunity for alignment of organisational and personal career goal achievement
- a minimum of inter-group conflict based on race, gender, nationality and other identity groups of organisation members.

While both Thomas's (1991) and Cox's (1991) view of the diversity-oriented organisation are in line with our vision we wish to attempt to tie down in more concrete terms what the exact characteristics of such an organisation would be. Rather than present the outcomes we will focus on the features.

One step beyond: our MOSAIC vision

The thinking behind our vision stems firstly from our working definition of managing diversity (as outlined in Table 10.1) and logical inferences drawn from our experience and the diversity literature.

Table 10.1
A working definition of managing diversity

The basic concept of managing diversity accepts that the workforce consists of a diverse population of people. The diversity consists of visible and non-visible differences which will include factors such as sex, age, background, race, disability, personality and workstyle. It is founded on the premiss that harnessing these differences will create a productive environment in which everybody feels valued, where their talents are being fully utilised and in which organisational goals are met.

The chief characteristics of this diversity-oriented organisation are presented in Table 10.2. Each of these characteristics will be discussed in turn.

Table 10.2
*MOSAIC: the characteristics of the
diversity-oriented organisation*

- **M**ission and values
- **O**bjective and fair processes
- **S**killed workforce: aware and fair
- **A**ctive flexibility
- **I**ndividual focus
- **C**ulture that empowers

Mission and values

The diversity-oriented organisation will have a strong, positive mission and core values which make managing diversity a necessary long-term business objective for the organisation and a responsibility of all employees. The values must reflect the personal and work needs of all employees.

Where diversity exists in an organisation and is allowed to flourish there also needs to be a core similarity (Shepard 1964) and this similarity must be focused upon agreement on the mission and values of the organisation. Without such a focus what has been referred to as the 'Balkanisation' (Gordon 1992) of the organisation could occur, that is, a fragmentation of individuals into cliques and separate in-groups/out-groups, with tension and conflict between them.

Extensive research on these group categorisations has been carried out (Messick and Mackie 1989; Fiske and Neuberg 1990). It has been established that every individual categorises others in terms of in-group/out-group. This categorisation is automatic and usually based at first on factors over which individuals have no control, for example age, sex, race, accent or attractiveness. The negative effects associated with this in-group/out-group categorisation are widely cited (Allport 1954; Tajfel 1970; Allison and Messick 1985; Wilder 1986).

However, there are a multitude of social categories beyond our physical features and research has shown that the potential exists for people to shift their categorisations to more psychological features (Brewer 1979). Allison and Herlocker (1994: 645) propose that a diversity-oriented organisation should introduce strategies that 'take advantage of this malleability' and in doing so produce an organisation-wide sense of in-group identity while at the same time recognising and appreciating diversity.

One of their suggestions on how to achieve this is the formation of 'superordinate' goals which require close and equal co-operation among members of differing groups. All employees need to feel that they are reliant on one another for success. Research has indicated that superordinate goals are effective in inducing people to view more positively individuals previously categorised as out-group (Stephan, Presser, Kennedy and Aronson 1978); in promoting inter-group harmony (Aronson and Osherow 1980); and in directing attention towards people's similarities rather than their differences (Gaertner *et al.* 1990).

It is our belief that these superordinate goals can be achieved through a strong alignment of managing diversity with the core organisational values – values which are, as Gottfredson (1992: 302) puts it, 'overarching [and] group-neutral . . . which members of diverse groups can subscribe and work toward together'.

Objective and fair processes

All the processes and systems (for example, recruitment, selection, induction, performance appraisals etc) will have been audited and are continually re-audited to ensure that no one age group, sex, ethnicity, or type predominates at any one level. Hindrances to diversity have been removed and the tools and techniques for assessment are regularly examined to ensure no other techniques are available that are more objective or fair.

As suggested by Gordon *et al.* (1991) particular attention should be paid during induction to ensuring that all employees are properly oriented into the organisation. This orientation should not be left to chance; rather, formal programmes such as mentoring should be in place and the informal networks of the organisation should be outlined. Actively orienting new employees into the organisation serves not only to ease their transition but also aids what Cox (1991) called the full integration of groups into the formal and informal networks of the organisation.

The criteria for selection and advancement will be openly available to everyone: it is not a guessing game. All employees should know not only when a vacancy arises but also the competencies and skills necessary for the post. An excellent example of a diversity-oriented selection system is that operated by Xerox (Sessa 1992). As part of Xerox's plan to manage diversity they instituted a process to ensure the movement of *all* employees who had both the ability and motivation into the upper levels of the organisation. One part of this process included giving employees the right to request a panel interview if they felt they were ready to progress into the managerial ranks. All employees were provided with the criteria for selection into management. This acted as a form of self-assessment, with employees requesting an interview when they felt they had met the requirements.

This type of system ensures that promotion is on merit alone and that all employees have an equal chance of moving up through the ranks. It also takes power away from any informal networks that may operate, networks that perpetuate the 'it's not what you know, it's who you know' style of selection and promotion.

Skilled workforce: aware and fair

There are two elements to this characteristic. First, it involves having a workforce aware of and guided by the principles of managing diversity. Second, it requires having managers who manage.

Aware and fair workforce.   Everyone in the organisation is dedicated to managing diversity. They understand why diversity is important and what they have to do to make it a reality. All employees have been trained to recognise how their biases and prejudices can influence their decisions and actions and are knowledgeable about the ways to prevent this happening. Employees recognise the value of teamwork and are skilled at working in teams. They are open to new ways of working.

Managers who manage. In the diversity-oriented organisation the emphasis should be on *the managing, not the diversity.* Our thinking here is in line with Thomas (1992) who places the focus of managing diversity very much on managerial capability. Thomas believes it is the lack of managerial competence rather than racism or sexism that may be the cause of managers' inability to manage diverse groups of people.

Managers will actively develop both themselves and their employees. All managers will ensure that they are constantly developing and acquiring new skills where appropriate. They will keep up to date with developments in the field and communicate this information to all employees. Managers will solicit feedback on their performance and will act upon it.

A good example of this happening in practice comes (again) from Xerox (Sessa 1992). They established a process – the Management Resources Process (MRP) – which focused on upward mobility and essentially required each manager to complete a personal history form, indicating their career development goals. They then underwent a group assessment with their supervisor and peers which culminated in feedback and the production of a development plan. Xerox are thus ensuring that they harness the potential of all employees from entry level to senior management.

Xerox also adhere to the principle that it is the managing that is crucial, not the diversity. They did initially, however, adopt a narrower focus but learnt from this experience. At an early stage of Xerox's approach to managing diversity the organisation set up a sensitivity awareness programme for managers. The programme was not a success: managers were indeed made aware of their biases but they were left unsure how to change them. The Management Practices Programme (MPP) was then introduced which gave managers tools and procedures for managing *everyone.* This programme was a success and is still running (Sessa 1992).

Managers skilled at making people feel valued will know how to harness potential whether they are dealing with a team of white males or one that is more mixed in terms of gender, ethnicity etc. They understand individual motivation and appraise employees with an understanding that people are not clones and should not be treated or assessed as such.

Development will not be left to chance. Managers will conduct performance appraisals with all their employees, developing and implementing career development plans on a regular basis. The ultimate aim of all managers is to maximise the potential of all their employees in order to meet organisational goals. Managers are therefore accountable for both their own development and that of their employees. As stated in Chapter 6 it is important that it is their managerial capability that is appraised, not how many diversity initiatives they have put in place. Pepsi-Cola International is an example of an organisation with this approach in appraising their managers.

In their quest to manage a diverse workforce Pepsi-Cola International have developed a task-oriented, culture-neutral organisational climate that stresses excellence in individual and team performance (Fulkerson and Schuler 1992). One process they have employed in order to achieve this excellence is people management accountability in all managerial appraisals. There are eight components to the accountability process:

- conducting performance appraisals: all managers must thoroughly evaluate the performance of their staff in a culturally neutral manner
- conducting personal development discussions: all managers must develop their subordinates using available performance management tools and have regular feedback discussions
- implementing developmental plans: development plans must be followed up to have the desired outcome
- attracting/hiring superior talent: each manager has responsibility for bringing talent into the organisation
- providing instant feedback/coaching: all ideas or problems relating to the business or an individual's performance are raised
- fostering teamwork: managers must co-operate and share knowledge with others

- building-bench: managers must ensure that talent is developed and prepared for greater responsibility
- managing/building executional excellence: ultimately, the bottom-line results must be delivered.

Active flexibility

There will be increased flexibility in the diversity-oriented organisation not only in terms of working patterns but also in all policies, practices and procedures.

Following Hall and Parker (1993), we would expect the diversity-oriented organisation to broaden the notion of flexibility to include the needs of all employees, not just those with families. For example, many organisations provide assistance with childcare, a benefit only for those employees with families. In our view a fairer approach would be to provide a 'cafeteria' of benefits from which employees select those most suitable for their needs. In this way it is the work/life needs of an employee that are addressed rather than only the work/family needs.

Flexibility will also be present in the way work is carried out. Existing norms will be challenged. Where possible the emphasis will be on the output rather than the number of hours worked. If an employee wants to work between 4 pm and 11 pm, and this does not interfere with colleagues or customers, then those are the hours that that employee should work.

British trade unions have demonstrated a willingness to accept flexible working conditions, but only when these new patterns of work are of genuine interest and benefit to their members. In order to ensure that flexible working does not lead to the deterioration of the terms and conditions of employment a set of guidelines has been developed (Staedelin 1986: x).

New patterns of work must:

- not be harmful to workers' health
- be subject to collective agreement
- have a positive effect on employment

- benefit from social security protection
- respect the basic rights of social and family life
- provide guarantees regarding wages and salaries
- include entitlement to annual holidays and weekly rest
- allow workers to achieve their potential.

These guidelines could be applied more broadly to all flexible approaches in an organisation, thus ensuring that flexibility is a benefit for all rather than a weapon used by employers.

Flexibility does not mean that separate policies and systems must be established for every different need recognised in the organisation; rather, it entails being flexible enough to respond to these needs if they are valid. Coopers & Lybrand in the USA have made this distinction clear in their approach to managing diversity: 'flexible simplicity'. The analogy they use for their approach is that of a paint shop which only stocks three primary colours and yet can provide a customer with any paint colour they want. By having the flexibility to combine the three colours the shop need not stock all possible colours. Their aim is not to create policies individually geared to specific groups (eg women) but rather to create a simple structure that can be flexibly applied to the needs of all employees (DeLuca and McDowell 1992).

It is important that flexibility does not become inflexible. This may appear to be a strange statement but the reality is that some organisations who believe they are flexible have in fact become inflexible in the other direction. One example is where an organisation changed its working patterns from being office-based to home-working. Employees had no say in this decision and either had to accept it or leave. Ironically, this organisation actually thought it was moving with the times to a more flexible approach.

The diversity-oriented organisaton recognises the diverse needs of employees and responds by providing a flexible approach, one that will enable the potential of all employees to be maximised. Furthermore, it will demonstrate that their differences have been accepted by the organisation and they are not expected to conform to a set of patterns and regulations laid down by the predominant culture.

Individual focus

This characteristic can be conceived as the overarching principle of all actions in a diversity-oriented organisation.

There are a number of initiatives that have been advocated by diversity writers as an essential part of managing diversity. While many of these initiatives conform with our mosaic vision of the diversity-oriented organisation (eg skills training, flexible work patterns), there are some that conflict. The conflicting initiatives are essentially those that have groups as their main focus rather than individuals.

Examples of these group-focused initiatives include corporately assigned 'special events' that focus on a particular group (eg 'black history week'); corporately designated core groups or caucuses that segregate groups; and training that focuses on highlighting the 'differences' between groups. Our contention is that such initiatives contradict the principles of managing diversity and are not an essential part of a diversity-oriented organisation. (In the name of flexibility, however, we would envision these initiatives taking place but only as an *employee-initiated and -driven* action.) The rationale behind our objections can be illustrated with the following examples.

It is often the case that organisations strive to sensitise employees to differences among various ethnic groups and to eradicate negative stereotypes by holding one- or two-day awareness courses that serve to point out the differences between groups. However, these courses run the risk of not only ingraining stereotypes even further but also of creating new, more powerful, stereotypes that simply replace the old ones. Such courses could result in increasing hostility and misunderstanding (Ellis and Sonnenfeld 1994; Hewstone and Brown 1986). Furthermore, Pettigrew (1986) and Hewstone and Brown (1986) have all argued that the positive effects of interracial contact will only develop cumulatively over time, and not as a result of one training course.

A number of organisations have already recognised this possibility and have also realised that individual differences rather than group differences should be the focus of attention. As a corporate policy Xerox do not provide special training to particular groups; as Sessa (1992: 60) asserts, they 'realised that many "minority" and "women" concerns were no different from concerns of white male majority population'.

Coopers & Lybrand, in adopting their 'flexible simplicity' approach, chose not to establish special programmes for women (DeLuca and McDowell 1992). They gave the following reasons for their decision:

- female professionals themselves would be likely to resist it
- to avoid perceptions of favouritism and backlash
- a belief that the issues are relevant to the entire workforce rather than being 'female professional' issues.

Ellis and Sonnenfeld (1994: 99) recommend that cross-cultural training programmes should be 'orientated toward fostering respect for employees as individual actors rather than toward treatment of employees as members of groups with easily categorised differences'.

It is sometimes the case that such an 'individual' approach evolves from a failed 'group' approach. As Gottfredson (1992: 286) recognises: 'The broadening of focus to include all employees often results from the limitations or side effects of the narrower focus.' Digital is a case in point.

Digital's 'valuing differences' approach to managing diversity emphasises personal development through discussion groups. These are known as core groups, and when they were established the focus was primarily on women and ethnic minorities. Gradually the groups realised this focus was inappropriate in that it 'merely reinforced the prevailing "us versus them" approach to AA/EEO, [affirmative action/equal employment opportunities] which made everyone feel devalued' (Walker and Hanson 1992: 125). The focus then evolved into one that explored group as well as individual differences in terms of race and gender. This soon expanded in turn into a focus including age, physical ability and sexual orientation. But as more and more employees from different parts of the organisation joined the groups the focus shifted yet again to all the ways

individuals differ eg job role, perspectives, learning styles etc.
These core groups still meet on a voluntary basis to learn more
about their individual differences and similarities.

Ellis and Sonnenfeld (1994: 90), reporting the experiences of
diversity initiatives in three organisations, describe one organisation's corporate response. GCI (a fictional name) run a series of
'corporate presentations and events that highlight the special
qualities and/or history of a particular ethnic group'. The
example given is a day when Polish food is served in the cafeteria
and information on Polish culture is distributed to staff. As Ellis
and Sonnenfeld rightly point out, while the intention may be to
enhance understanding there is a big risk that such initiatives will
appear patronising or offensive and perhaps perpetuate cultural
stereotypes.

As previously stated we believe that if employees want to set up
their own segregated groups or if they want to run special events
celebrating one particular group's culture then organisations should
respond favourably. Such initiatives should not however be corpo-
rate-led.

Xerox adopted this approach, and employee-driven rather than
corporate-initiated caucuses have been established. They are totally
autonomous and meet in their own time. While there are quite a
number of caucus groups, each focusing on one particular group, it
is interesting to note that they have never collaborated on any projects (Sessa 1992). Could it be that such groups facilitate segrega-
tion rather than encourage co-operation and integration?

It is our opinion that, whether they are favourable or not, aver-
aging group similarities or differences contradicts a managing
diversity perspective. The diversity-oriented organisation focuses
on developing and promoting all employees, not on highlighting
group differences. Xerox, Pepsi-Cola International and Coopers &
Lybrand have realised this.

Culture that empowers

The basic assumptions underlying all activity in an organisation are
incorporated in its culture. The diversity-oriented organisation must

ensure this culture is consistent and complementary to managing diversity.

Thomas (1994: 61) describes the diversity-oriented organisation as one that eliminates 'the subtle and not-so-subtle roadblocks to participation and creativity that can exist if a diverse workforce is hampered by a culture bound to the ethics, practices and customs of the monocultural (usually white and male) hierarchy that was present at its inception'. In our view the old culture should not only be eliminated but an empowering culture must be created.

The diversity-oriented organisation understands the importance of organisational culture and how this affects individuals within it. As a result it will ensure that all employees have an understanding of how the organisation operates, what it values and how it expects its employees to behave.

In our view an empowering culture will encapsulate the following elements:

- There will be an open, trusting environment in which there is an absence of prejudice and discrimination.
- There will be an acceptance that resources such as jobs, income and access to information are distributed equally. Key projects or responsibilities are allocated on merit alone.
- Managing diversity is viewed as a business objective.
- Decision making will be devolved to the lowest point possible.
- Participation and consultation will be encouraged and management will listen to and act on what employees are saying. There is recognition that valuable ideas can come from below; as one organisation we have worked for put it 'with every pair of hands you get a free brain'.
- All employees understand the core values.
- There is open communication and an open flow of information throughout the organisation within and between all levels. Business goals are clearly communicated to everyone. An 'us (employees)/them (management)' culture is discouraged.
- The need for experimentation is valued and encouraged; people are allowed to fail. Gordon et al. (1991) believe that stretching assignments should be given to all new employees early in their

careers and that managers should not let their personal stereotypes prevent some employees from getting a chance to show
how good they are.
• Innovation and creativity are fostered.

The diversity-oriented organisation and the learning organisation: two visions overlap

There is considerable overlap between the vision of the diversity-
oriented organisation and that of 'the learning organisation'. Both
managing diversity and learning organisation theory are striving to
create organisations in which the potential of all employees is
valued and optimised, the ultimate aim being the creation of a more
satisfying and productive environment in which organisational
goals are met and indeed surpassed. However, quite different
approaches have been adopted to achieve this vision. It is our view
that these approaches should be conceived as complementary rather
than competing strategies: there are few advantages to be gained
from keeping them separate but many benefits to be realised from a
united approach. In this section we will outline both the similarities
and the differences between managing diversity and the learning
organisation and we will also present our *symbiotic model* of the
way forward. First a brief overview of current thinking on the
learning organisation will be outlined.

The learning organisation

A great deal has been written about the learning organisation and
many organisations have been keen to adopt and implement learning
organisation theory (Senge 1990; Pedler, Burgoyne and Boydell,
1992; Dixon 1994; Argyris 1990; Garratt 1990). Organisations
have been quick to realise that the capacity to learn at an individual,
group and organisational level is critical if they are to have the

ability to respond to an increasingly unpredictable future. As Stata (1989: 64) asserted: 'the rate at which individuals and organisations learn may become the only sustainable competitive advantage'.

The Pearn Kandola approach to the learning organisation will be outlined so as to enable a comparison to be made with managing diversity. The Pearn Kandola model avoids a prescriptive definition of the learning organisation. Instead a *working approach* was developed that can be adapted or used as a springboard by organisations and a *six-factor model* has been outlined that facilitates organisational self-analysis.

The working approach incorporates five components (see Table 10.3). The emphasis is on ensuring that not only are *enhancers* to learning put in place but also that *inhibitors* to learning arc identified and eliminated. These inhibitors and enhancers can operate at an individual or group level; they can also function structurally or organisationally.

Table 10.3
The Pearn Kandola working approach to the
learning organisation

> - A learning organisation places high value on individual and organisational learning as a prime asset.
> - It works towards full utilisation of all individual and group potential for learning and adapts itself to meet (and eventually set and review) organisational objectives.
> - It does this in a way that also satisfies the needs and aspirations of the people involved.
> - Inhibitors or blocks to learning are identified and removed while strong enhancers and structural support for sustained continuous learning are put in place.
> - A climate of continuous learning and improvement is created.

A six-factor model for a learning organisation

The Pearn Kandola *six-factor model* for a learning organisation enables organisations to identify their learning inhibitors and enhancers and helps them pinpoint those areas where action is required. The six factors are defined as follows.

Shared vision: the extent to which there is a vision already in place that includes the organisation's capacity to identify, respond to and benefit from future possibilities; part of this vision recognises the importance of learning at individual, group and system level to enable the organisation to transform itself continuously in order not only to survive but also thrive in an increasingly unpredictable world.

Enabling structure: the extent to which the organisation has been designed and operates to facilitate learning between different levels, functions and subsystems; also the recognition of the need for rapid adaptation and change.

Supportive culture: the extent to which expressed values and displayed behaviour by the organisation's leaders encourage challenges to the status quo, the questioning of assumptions and established ways of doing things; also the provision of opportunities for testing, experimenting and for continuous development. Exploration and debate are valued commodities, and mistakes are treated positively.

Empowering management: the extent to which managers genuinely believe that devolved decision making and autonomous teamworking result in improved performance by those much closer to the work actually done and/or the customer. Managers see their role as facilitating and coaching rather than controlling and monitoring.

Motivated workforce: the extent to which the workforce as a whole is motivated to learn continuously, is confident to take on new learning and seize opportunities for learning from experience, and is fully committed to self-development.

Enhanced learning: the extent to which the organisation has processes and policies to enhance, encourage and sustain learning amongst all employees.

Similarities between the diversity-oriented organisation and the learning organisation

As outlined above both the diversity-oriented organisation and the learning organisation share the common aim of optimising the potential of *all* employees for the benefit of the organisation. There are a number of other similarities that can be identified between the two approaches (see Table 10.4). Both require a change in organisational culture, ways of working and management.

The business case for realising the potential of all employees clearly underlies both approaches. The central idea behind the learning organisation is that unless organisations increase their capacity to learn then they not only run the risk of losing out to competitors but they may not even survive. A similar argument has been presented for managing diversity. The need for a strategic approach is advocated, whereby strong links are to be forged with the business objectives.

Table 10.4

Similarities between managing diversity and the learning organisation

- ultimate aim
- driven by business case
- empowering culture
- manager as coach
- devolved decision making
- teamworking
- people-driven

Both approaches require a move towards a more empowering culture where individuals are afforded the right to determine how they carry out their work – a culture where control is taken away from management, and innovation and creativity are fostered through increased autonomy.

In both the diversity-oriented organisation and the learning organisation a great deal of importance is placed on teamworking. The value of teams is recognised and employees are encouraged to manage themselves. Decision making is also devolved to the lowest point possible, thus avoiding a 'management knows best' culture.

Managerial capability is central to both approaches. It is essential that managers respond to the needs of employees and recognise that no one approach is necessarily correct. In the diversity-oriented organisation, as in the learning organisation, managers are seen as coaches: their role is to empower rather than command employees, to unleash rather than stifle potential.

Differences between the diversity-oriented organisation and the learning organisation

There are a number of ways in which the two approaches differ (see Table 10.5). What appears to make the diversity approach unique, for example, is the way it enables organisations to manage effectively those employees who may be in a minority – people who have stereotyping to deal with and who may be discriminated against. It is noticeable that the literature on the learning organisation makes very little reference to bias, discrimination and prejudice. The tools of the learning organisation focus instead on optimising learning, be it at the individual, group or organisational level.

The learning organisation adopts a longer-term approach, striving to improve current performance while at the same time *creating* the future for the organisation. It is this 'proactive' future orientation that separates the approach from managing diversity. In the main, the diversity-oriented organisation has current performance as its central focus, although that is not to suggest that in doing so it is not creating an organisation that is more responsive to change, in essence a 'reactive' future orientation.

Table 10.5
Differences between managing diversity and the learning organisation

– the tools they provide
– time-scales
– targets for change
– change of mindsets

While both approaches advocate a change in culture, systems and managerial skills, managing diversity differs in the importance it places in auditing all processes in terms of their objectivity and fairness. The learning organisation, on the other hand, aims to introduce new working methods that enable the organisation to learn more effectively.

There is also a subtle difference in the change in mindset required for both approaches. The diversity-oriented organisation requires a move away from a focus on groups to a focus on individuals, while the learning organisation shifts the emphasis from training which is 'done to you' to learning which is 'learner-led'.

Diversity and learning: a symbiotic model

The link between the two approaches is summarised in Table 10.6.

Table 10.6
A complementary approach

- **Managing diversity**: maximises the pool of potential in an organisation
- **The learning organisation**: harnesses the potential in this pool
- **The aim**: realising the potential of all employees

Managing diversity not only ensures there is a diverse pool of potential available within the organisation but also releases this potential and begins the learning process. But managing diversity has little to say about doing things in new ways eg adopting a learner-led approach as opposed to traditional training. In order for the full potential of all employees to be utilised a learning organisation approach is required.

The learning organisation enables the full utilisation of all potential, but if the organisation is not diversity-oriented there is a risk that the available pool of potential will be narrow. The learning organisation therefore needs to ensure the organisation is successfully managing diversity.

The need for a complementary approach can be captured in dia-
grammatic form (see Figures 10.1 and 10.2). The current approach
(Figure 10.1) is one in which managing diversity and the learning
organisation are seen as competing strategies ie two separate circles
both striving for the same vision ie realising the potential of all
employees.

Figure 10.1
Managing diversity and the learning organisation:
the current approach

The symbiotic approach, however, not only ensures that *all the
available potential* within an organisation is realised but also that
the pool of potential incorporates *all the possible potential* available to the organisation (Figure 10.2). Managing diversity maximises the potential and in doing so increases the available pool of
potential for the learning organisation by pushing out the bound-
aries of the circle. It is this increased pool of potential that is harnessed, resulting in the realisation of all possible potential (the
outer circle). Adopting this symbiotic approach, as can be seen
from Figure 10.2, ensures that the potential realised is constantly
being magnified.

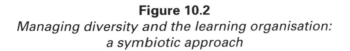

Figure 10.2
*Managing diversity and the learning organisation:
a symbiotic approach*

Managing diversity has benefits to offer in recruiting, retaining and getting the best from *all* the workforce, which includes not making assumptions about people based on superficial ideas of their group membership. The learning organisation has benefits in how to ensure you are optimising the learning capacity in this workforce.

There appears to be considerable scope for writers on diversity to tackle issues relating to the learning organisation yet with few exceptions (eg Hall and Parker 1993) these connections have been missed. Managing diversity should not be seen as separate from the learning organisation; it should instead be striving to refresh such approaches with the principles of diversity by adopting a symbiotic approach.

Key points

- In this chapter we have taken one step beyond and have out-
  lined our Mosaic Vision of the diversity-oriented organisation.
- The mosaic vision has six characteristics:
  - **M**ission and values
  - **O**bjective and fair processes
  - **S**killed workforce: aware and fair
  - **A**ctive flexibility
  - **I**ndividual focus
  - **C**ulture that empowers.
- The links between the diversity-oriented organisation and the
  learning organisation are also made explicit. The value of
  adopting an integrated approach is highlighted in our symbi-
  otic model of both approaches.

11

The Final Piece: Completing the Picture

Throughout this book we have explored and critically examined the concept of managing diversity. In our view diversity is a necessary evolutionary step in the implementation of equal opportunities; it represents an overarching organisational strategy that expands beyond current equal opportunities thinking by concentrating on the realisation of the potential of *all* employees at all levels of the organisation (see Table 11.1).

Table 11.1
How managing diversity is different

MANAGING DIVERSITY	EQUAL OPPORTUNITIES
– ensures all employees maximise their potential and their contribution to the organisation	– concentrates on discrimination
– embraces a broad range of people; no one is excluded	– is perceived as an issue for women, ethnic minorities and people with disabilities
– concentrates on movement within an organisation, the culture of the organisation and the meeting of business objectives	– concentrates on the numbers of groups employed
– is the concern of all employees, especially managers	– is seen as an issue to do with personnel and human resource practitioners
– does not rely on positive action/affirmative action.	– relies on positive action.

However, we have not merely accepted all that is touted in the name of diversity. We hope instead to have forged our own view of

173

the way forward. In doing so many new and interesting findings have been unearthed from beneath previously unturned stones. Specifically we have looked at what is good in managing diversity, what the dangers of diversity are, what is supportable in the claims for diversity, what progress has been made in the UK and, above all, why diversity is a necessary and essential strategy for organisations. A number of important findings emerged at each stage of our analysis – the key points of these findings have been made explicit in each chapter but they warrant reiteration here.

Looking beneath the surface

Two areas that yielded very illuminating data when examined more closely related to the benefits to be achieved from diversity and the skills necessary to manage diversity. A clear picture of the reality only emerged after careful inspection of the available evidence.

Many benefits have been claimed to result from effectively managing diversity. Our examination of these supposed benefits highlighted the inconclusiveness of the supporting data, particularly for what we have termed the debatable and indirect benefits. The evidence was found to be very sketchy in places and non-existent in others. In our view it is therefore necessary to invest more time and energy into substantiating these claims rather than simply overstating the gains. If we do not, we run the risk of diluting the proven direct benefits that exist and perhaps discrediting the whole area of managing diversity.

Several writers on diversity have suggested the need for what they term a diversity competence. Upon examination it was discovered that the skills necessary to manage diversity are essentially a restatement of an old theme, namely good interpersonal or communication skills. It is these skills that need to be emphasised in training managers in the diversity-oriented organisation. Good managers of diversity are essentially just that – good managers, and good managers are those who deal with employees as individuals rather than expect everyone to be equally motivated and to work in the same way. Managers must be made aware of the importance of diversity and should be rewarded for both the development of all their staff and for self-development.

New perspectives

New data on diversity initiatives in the UK and innovative ideas on how to manage diversity have also been established. These new perspectives provide both a clear starting-point and a springboard for action.

Our own research into current UK practice provided some interesting results. Among the most revealing was that many organisations still have a traditional equal opportunities approach, with the focus on specific groups, yet the initiatives perceived to be the most successful were those related to the needs of *all* employees rather than groups. Are organisations ignoring such data or is it that they have not carried out a proper analysis of the data they have themselves collected? We suspect the latter – our research suggests that even the evaluation itself is piecemeal. Organisations need to move away from this 'initiatives for initiatives' sake' mentality to a more business-led, strategic approach.

Our strategic implementation model is, to our knowledge, the first to be validated, and as such has been shown to be related to successful implementation of diversity initiatives. The validation of models is necessary if we are to provide organisations with a solid framework for managing their diversity. The experiences of IDV have been presented as an illustration of a UK organisation that has successfully embarked on the strategic implementation of diversity.

The symbiotic model of the link between managing diversity and the learning organisation provides a fresh conceptualisation of the benefits to be gained from synthesising diversity with other change initiatives. This model is a potent reminder of the benefits to be gained from realising the potential of *all* employees, not just a subset. We should not restrict ourselves to a blinkered view of diversity, rather we should see it as offering a new synthesis of ideas richer than previous notions.

Individuals not groups

The focus of our MOSAIC vision of the diversity-oriented organ-isation is very much at the individual level. While we acknowledge there are average differences between groups, for example cultural differences, we believe that the similarities between groups are of equal if not greater importance. By adopting an individual approach the needs of all employees can be realised and the possibility of excluding those individuals who do not fall into typical groupings eliminated. An open, objective and fair organisation is not one that downplays or elevates group differences but one in which these differences can thrive.

A group-focused approach carries with it many dangers. There is a risk that stressing the differences between groups will lead to the strengthening of stereotypes and the belief that all individuals in any one group conform to this stereotype. New stereotypes may also be created that are stronger than those previously held. Prefer-ential treatment for groups, such as positive action or the formation of special segregated committees or events, can result in resentment among those excluded and a lack of self-esteem and feelings of inadequacy in the recipients.

Processes and systems

In our vision of the diversity-oriented organisation recruitment, selection, promotion, training, work allocation and management are all geared to responding to the individual needs of employees. It is the management that is important, not the diversity. The recruit-ment, selection and promotion processes need to be audited and reaudited to ensure their fairness. The focus of diversity training should not be to emphasise the differences between groups but to highlight the importance of diversity ie both the differences *and* the similarities.

A flexible approach is paramount in the diversity-oriented organisation. Organisations will need to move away from a narrow focus of flexibility, responsive only to those groups perceived to need it. Again it is the needs of all employees that should be catered for, not their group membership. Just as flexible working hours are not the sole domain of women so other flexible initiatives should not be targeted at one specific group. A change in focus is also required: organisations need to move towards being employee-friendly rather than just family-friendly.

Being an employee in a diversity-oriented organisation requires listening, questioning, challenging and acknowledging. It is necessary actively to *listen* to the views of other employees, to *question* your own stereotypes and ways of working, to *challenge* the existing norms, working methods and initiatives in the organisation (including those that fall under the banner of managing diversity) and to *acknowledge* that no one style of working is invariably the right one.

Managing diversity could represent the start of an exciting voyage of exploration. It is a new, dynamic and evolving area; no one finite set of ideas on how to manage diversity can be said to hold true in all circumstances. Rather, like employees in the diversity-oriented organisation, those of us in the diversity field must also listen, question, challenge and acknowledge the different viewpoints on how to manage diversity. We must remain open to opinions that are uncomfortable or present different ways forward. If we do not, our vision will be limited and our journey short.

 **Appendix**

Breakdown of respondents by organisational sector

Organisational Sector	n*	%
Manufacturing	52	21.6
Retail	12	5.0
Finance and Insurance	19	7.9
Transport	7	2.9
Media/Publishing	8	3.3
Communications	7	2.9
Construction	9	3.75
Local Government	44	18.3
Civil Service	20	8.3
Public Services	5	2.08
Health	27	11.25
Education	15	6.25
Utilities	12	5.0
Leisure	3	1.25

* n = 240 owing to missing data.

Breakdown of respondents by employee mix

Women (%)	n*	%
1–25	53	20.0
26–50	89	33.6
51–75	83	31.3
76–100	40	15.1
Ethnic Minorities (%)		
0	27	11.6
1–5	136	58.4
6–15	49	21.0
16–100	21	9.0
People with Disabilities (%)		
0	30	12.6
1	106	44.4
2–3	77	32.2
4–100	26	10.9

* n varies owing to missing data.

References

ABASSI S. M. and HOLLMAN K. W. (1991) 'Managing cultural diversity: the challenge of the 90's. *ARMA Records Management Quarterly*, 25, 24–32.

ADLER N. (1986). *International Dimensions of Organisational Behaviour*. Boston, Kent Publishing.

ALLISON S. T. and HERLOCKER C. E. (1994). 'Constructing impressions in demographically diverse organizational settings. (Impression Management and Diversity: issues for organizational behaviour).' *American Behavioral Scientist*, 37, 5, 637–52.

ALLISON S. T. and MESSICK D. M. (1985) 'The group attribution error'. *Journal of Experimental Social Psychology*, 21, 563–79.

ALLPORT G. W. (1954). *The Nature of Prejudice*. Reading, MA, Addison-Wesley.

ANDERSON L. R. (1966). 'Leader behaviour, member attitudes and task performance of intercultural discussion groups.' *Journal of Social Psychology*, 69, 305–19.

ANDERSON L. R. (1983) 'Management of the mixed-cultural work group.' *Organizational Behaviour and Human Performance*, 31, 303–30.

Argyris C. (1962). *Interpersonal Competence and Organisational Effectiveness*. Homewood, IL, the Dorsey Press.

ARGYRIS C. (1990). *Overcoming Organisational Defences: Facilitating Organisational Learning*. Boston, MA, Allyn and Bacon.

ARONSON E. and OSHEROW N. (1980). 'Cooperation, prosocial behaviour and academic performance: experiments in the desegregated classroom.' *Applied Social Psychology Annual*, 1, 163–96.

ARVEY R. D. and FALEY R. H. (1988). *Fairness in Selecting Employees*. (Second edition.) Reading, MA, Addison-Wesley.

BARNOUW V. (1969). In Ross Webber, *Culture and Management*. Homewood, Richard D. Irwin.

BARTLETT C. A. and GHOSHAL S. (1989). *Managing across Borders: the Transnational Solution*. Boston, MA, Harvard Business School Preview.

BARTRAM D. (1992). 'The personality of UK managers'. *Journal of Occupational and Organisational Psychology*, 65, 2, 159–73.

BARTZ D. E., HILLMAN L. W., LEHRER S. and MAYHUGH G. M. (1990). 'A model for managing workforce diversity'. *Management Education and Development*, 21, 5, 321–6.

BAUER T. N. and GREEN S. G. (1994). 'Effect of newcomer involvement in work-related activities: a longitudinal study of socialisation'. *Journal of Applied Psychology*, 79, 2, 211–23.

BELBIN R. M. (1981). *Management Teams: Why They Succeed or Fail.* Oxford, Heinemann Professional Publishing Ltd.

BELL D. (1973). *The Coming of Post-industrial Society: a Venture in Social Forecasting.* New York, Basic Books.

BERRY-LOUND D. J. (1993). *A Carer's Guide to Eldercare.* Horsham, The Host Consultancy.

BETTENHAUSEN K. L. (1991). 'Five years of groups research: what we have learned and what needs to be addressed'. *Journal of Management*, 17, 2, 345–81.

BONHAM-CARTER M. (1991). 'The making of a cultural mosaic'. *The Guardian*, 30 December.

BOURANTAS D. and PAPALEXANDRIS N. (1990). 'Sex differences in leadership'. *Journal of Managerial Psychology*, 5, 5, 7–11.

BOWSER B. P. (1988). 'Defining corporate culture: exploring the relations between values, decision-making and cultural diversity.' Conference paper, American Sociological Association.

BRAHAM J. (1989). 'No, you don't manage everyone the same'. *Industry Week*, 238, 28–35.

BREWER M. B. (1979). 'In-group bias in the minimal intergroup situation: a cognitive motivational analysis'. *Psychological Bulletin*, 86, 307–24.

BREWSTER C. and HEGEWISCH A. (1993). 'A continent of diversity'. *Personnel Management*, January, 36–40.

BROADNAX W. D. (1991). 'From civil rights to valuing diversity'. *The Bureaucrat*, 20, 9–13.

BROWN L. D. (1983). *Managing Conflict at Organisational Interfaces.* Reading, MA, Addison-Wesley.

BUHLER P. (1993). 'Understanding cultural diversity and its benefits.' *Supervision*, 54, 7, 17–19.

BULLER P. F. (1986). 'The team building-task peformance relation: some conceptual and methodological refinements'. *Group and Organization Studies*, 11, 3, 147–68.

BURSTEIN P. (1992). 'Affirmative action, jobs and American democracy: what has happened to the quest for equal opportunity?' *Law and Society Review*, 26, 4, 905–22.

CALORI R. (1988). 'How successful companies manage diverse businesses'. *Long Range Planning (UK)*, June, 21, 3, 80–9.

CANNON F. (1993). 'Pre-recruitment training: the TSB experience'. *Equal Opportunities Review*, March/April, 48, 28–31.

CAPRA F. (1983). *The Turning Point.* London, Fontana.

CENTRE FOR RESEARCH IN ETHNIC RELATIONS (1993). *Ethnic Minorities in*

Great Britain: Age and Gender Structure. (1991 Census Statistical Paper No. 2.) University of Warwick, Coventry, CRER.

COLE S. (1990). 'Cultural diversity and sustainable futures'. *Futures (UK)*, 22, 10, 1044–58.

COMMISSION OF THE EUROPEAN COMMUNITIES (1992). *Social Europe: Equal Opportunities for Women and Men.* Luxembourg, Office for Official Publications for the Communities.

COMMISSION FOR RACIAL EQUALITY (1984). *Race Relations Code of Practice; for the Elimination of Racial Discrimination and the Promotion of Equality of Opportunity in Employment.* London, HMSO.

COMMISSION FOR RACIAL EQUALITY (1989). *Are Employers Complying?* London, CRE.

COPELAND L. (1988). 'Learning to manage a multicultural workforce'. *Training*, May, 48–56.

COX T. (1991). 'The multicultural organisation'. *Academy of Management Executive*, 5, 2, 34–47.

COX T. (1992). 'Can equal opportunity be made more equal?' *Harvard Business Review*, March–April, 141–42.

COX T. H. and BLAKE S. (1991). 'Managing cultural diversity: implications for organizational competitiveness.' *Academy of Management Executive*, 5, 45–56.

CROSBY F. and CLAYTON S. (1990). 'Affirmative action and the issue of expectancies.' *Journal of Social Issues*, 46, 2, 61–79.

CURSON C. (1988). *Flexible Patterns of Work.* London, Institute of Personnel Management.

DAVIDSON M. J. (1991). 'Women managers in Britain – issues for the 1990s'. *Women in Management Review*, 6, 1, 5–10.

DeLUCA J. M. and McDOWELL R. N. (1992). Managing Diversity: A Strategic 'Grass-Roots' Approach, in Jackson S. E. and Associates (1992), 227–47.

DEPARTMENT OF ECONOMIC DEVELOPMENT (1989). *Fair Employment in Northern Ireland.* Code of Practice. Belfast, DED.

DICKSON R. D. (1992). 'The business of equal opportunity'. *Harvard Business Review*, January–February, 46–53.

DIXON N. (1994). *The Organisational Learning Cycle.* Maidenhead, McGraw-Hill.

DOMINQUEZ C. M. (1991). 'The challenge of Workforce 2000'. *The Bureaucrat*, 20, 15–18.

DONALDSON, L. (1993). 'The recession: a barrier to equal opportunities?' *Equal Opportunities Review*, July–August, 50, 1–16.

DRAKE L. M. (1992). 'Can equal opportunities be made more equal?' *Harvard Business Review*, March–April, 142.

DREYFUSS J. (1990). 'Get ready for the new workforce'. *Fortune*, April.

ELLIS C. and SONNENFELD J. A. (1994). 'Diverse approaches to managing diversity'. *Human Resource Management*, 33, 1, 79–109.

ELLISON R. (1994). 'British labour force projections: 1994 to 2006'. *Employment Gazette*, April, 111–22.

EMPLOYMENT DEPARTMENT (1988). *Employment for the 1990s*. London, HMSO.

EQUAL OPPORTUNITIES COMMISSION (1985). *Code of Practice: Equal Opportunity Policies, Procedures and Practices in Employment*. London, HMSO.

EQUAL OPPORTUNITIES REVIEW (1993). 'Job advertising and the SDA'. *Equal Opportunities Review*, November–December, 52, 12–19.

ETHNIC MINORITY BUSINESS INITIATIVE (1991). *Ethnic Minority Business Development Team–Final Report, Action for Cities*. London, Home Office.

EUROLINK AGE (1993). *Age Discrimination against Older Workers in the EC*. London, Eurolink Age.

FALKENBERG, L. (1990). 'Improving the accuracy of stereotypes within the workplace'. *Journal of Management*, 16, 1, 107–18.

FERRARIO M. (1991). 'Sex differences in leadership style: myth or reality?' *Women in Management Review*. 6, 3, 16–21.

FISKE S. T. and NEUBERG S. L. (1990) 'A continuum of impression formation, from category-based to individuating processes: influences of information and motivation on attention and interpretation'. In M. P. Zanna (ed.), *Advances in Experimental Social Psychology*, 23, 1–74. New York, Academic Press.

FULKERSON J. R. and SCHULER R. S. (1992). Managing worldwide diversity at Pepsi-Cola International, in Jackson S. E. and Associates (1992), 248–78.

FULLERTON H. N. (1989). 'New labour force projections, spanning 1988 to 2000'. *Monthly Labour Review*, November, 3–11.

FULLERTON J. M. and BOYLE S. (1994). 'The rise of the assessment centre (AC): a survey of AC usage in the UK'. Paper presented at the 38th annual conference of the British Psychological Society, Northern Ireland Branch, April 1994.

GAERTNER S. L., MANN J. A., DOVIDIO J. F., MURRELL, A. J. and POMARE, M. (1990). 'How does cooperation reduce intergroup bias?' *Journal of Personality and Social Psychology*, 59, 692–704.

GALAGAN P. A. (1991). 'Tapping the power of a diverse workforce'. *Training and Development Journal*, 45, 3, 38–44.

GARRATT R. (1990). *Creating a Learning Organisation*. Cambridge, Director Books.

GOOLD M. and CAMPBELL A. (1987). 'Managing diversity: strategy and control in diversified British companies'. *Long Range Planning*, 20, 5, 42–52.

GORDON G. G., DiTOMASO N. and FARRIS G. F. (1991). 'Managing diversity in R and D groups'. *Research Technology Management*, January–February 34, 1, 18–23.

GORDON J. (1992). 'Rethinking diversity'. *Training*, January.

GOTTFREDSON L. S. (1992). Dilemmas in developing diversity programs, in Jackson S. E. and Associates (1992), 279–305.

GREENSLADE M. (1991). 'Managing diversity: lessons from the United States'. *Personnel Management*, December, 28–32.

HALL D. T. and PARKER V. A. (1993). "The role of workplace flexibility in managing diversity'. *Organisational Dynamics*, 22, 1, 4–18.

HAMMOND T. R. and KLEINER B. H. (1992). 'Managing multicultural work environments'. *Equal Opportunities International*, 11, 2, 6–9.

HAMMOND V. (1992). 'Opportunity 2000: a culture change approach to equal opportunity'. *Women in Management Review*, 7, 7, 3–10.

HAMMOND V. and HOLTON V. (1991). *A Balanced Workforce*. Ashridge, Management Research Group.

HARISIS D. S. and KLEINER B. H. (1993). 'Managing and valuing diversity in the workplace'. *Equal Opportunities International*, 12, 4, 6–9.

HARRE R. and LAMB, R. (1986). *The Dictionary of Personality and Social Psychology*. Oxford, Blackwell.

HARRINGTON L. (1993). 'Why managing diversity is so important'. *Distribution*, 92, 11, 88–92.

HEILMAN M. E. (1994). 'Affirmative action: some unintended consequences for working women'. *Research in Organizational Behaviour*, 16, 125–69.

HERRIOT P. (1989). *Recruitment in the 90s*. London, Institute of Personnel Management.

HEWSTONE M. and BROWN R. (1986). 'Contact is not enough: an intergroup perspective on the "contact hypothesis" '. In M. Hewstone and R. Brown (eds), *Contact and Conflict in Intergroup Encounters*, Oxford, Basil Blackwell.

HILL G. W. (1982). 'Group versus individual performance: are n + 1 heads better than one?' *Psychological Bulletin*, 91, 3, 517–39.

HOFFMAN L. R. and MAIER R. F. (1961). 'Quality and acceptance of problem solving by members of homogeneous and heterogenous groups'. *Journal of Abnormal and Social Psychology*, 62, 401–7.

HOFSTEDE G. (1984). *Culture's consequences: International Differences in Work-related Values*. Beverly Hills, Sage.

HOLLAND L. (1988). 'Easy to say, hard to do: managing an equal opportunity programme'. *Equal Opportunities Review*, 20, 16–21.

HONEY S., MEAGER N. and WILLIAMS M. (1993). *Employers Attitudes towards People with Disabilities*. Dorset, BEPC Ltd.

INDUSTRIAL RELATIONS SERVICES (1990). *Effective Ways of Recruiting and Retaining Women*. London, Industrial Relations Services.

INSTITUTE OF MANAGEMENT (1994). *National Management Survey: Remuneration Economics*. Corby, Institute of Management.

JACKSON S. E. (1992). Preview of the road to be travelled, in Jackson S. E. and Associates (1992), 3–12.

JACKSON S. E. and ALVAREZ E. B. (1992). Working through diversity as a strategic imperative, in Jackson S. E. and Associates (1992), 13–36.

JACKSON S. E. and ASSOCIATES (1992). *Diversity in the Workplace: Human Resource Initiatives*. (Society for Industrial and Organisational Psychology: the Professional Practice Series.) New York, The Guildford Press.

JAMIESON D. and O'MARA J. (1991). *Managing Workforce 2000: Gaining the Diversity Advantage*. San Francisco, Jossey-Bass.

JANIS I. (1972). *Victims of Groupthink*. Boston, MA, Houghton Mifflin.

JENKINS R. (1986). *Racism and Recruitment: Managers, Organisations and Equal Opportunity in the Labour Market*. Cambridge, Cambridge University Press.

JOHNSTON W. B. and PACKER A. H. (1987). *Workforce 2000: Work and Workers for the 21st Century*. Indianapolis, In, The Hudson Institute.

JONES JR. E. W. (1992). 'Can equal opportunity be made more equal?' *Harvard Business Review*, March-April, 155.

KANDOLA R. S. (1989). 'Using job analysis as a basis for selection'. In M. Smith and I. Robertson (eds), *Advances in Selection and Assessment*. Chichester, John Wiley and Sons.

KANTER R. M. (1977). *Men and Women of the Corporation*. New York, Basic Books.

KANTER R. M. (1983), *The Change Masters*. New York, Simon and Schuster.

KELLEY H. H. (1972). 'Attribution in Social Interaction'. In E. E. Jones, D. E. Kanouse, H. H. Kelley, R. E Nisbett, S. Valins and B. Weiner (eds), *Attribution: Perceiving the Causes of Behaviour*. Morristown, NJ, Learning Press.

KELLEY H. H. and MICHELA J. L. (1980). 'Attribution theory and research'. In M. Rosenzweig and L. Pater (eds), *Annual Review of Psychology*, 31, 457–501, Palo Alto, CA, Annual Reviews Inc.

KENNEDY J. and EVEREST A. (1991). 'Putting diversity into context'. *Personnel Journal*, September, 50–54.

KIM J. S. and CAMPAGNA A. F. (1981). 'Effects of flexitime on employee attendance and performance: a field experiment', *Academy of Management Journal*, December, 14, 729–41.

KOSSEK E. E. and ZONIA S. C. (1993) 'Assessing diversity climate: a field study to promote diversity'. *Journal of Organisational Behaviour*, 14, 61–81.

LOCAL GOVERNMENT MANAGEMENT BOARD (1993). *Equal Opportunities in*

Local Government: Equal Opportunities Survey of Local Authorities, Covering Policies, Measures and Monitoring. London, Local Government Management Board.

LYNCH F. R. (1994). 'Workforce diversity: PC's final frontier?' *National Review*, 46, 3, 32.

LYNCH F. R. and BEER W. R. (1990). 'You ain't the right colour, pal'. *Policy Review*, Winter, 64–7.

MANDRELL B. and KOHLER-GRAY (1990). 'Management development that values diversity'. *Personnel*, March, 67.

MARTIN J., MELTZER, H. and ELLIOT D. (1988). *The Prevalence of Disability among Adults.* London, HMSO.

MASON J. L. (1992). 'Can equal opportunity be made more equal?' *Harvard Business Review*, March–April, 146.

MASTERSON B. (1992). 'Bridging the culture gap'. *Human Resources*, Spring, 48–52.

McDONALD H. (1993). 'The diversity industry: cashing in on affirmative action'. *New Republic*, July 5, 209, 1, 22–5.

McENRUE M. P. (1993). 'Managing diversity: Los Angeles before and after the riots'. *Organisational Dynamics*, Winter, 21, 3, 18–29.

McGREGOR A. and SPROULL A. (1992). 'Employers and the flexible workforce'. *Employment Gazette*, May, 225–34.

McRAE S. (1989). *Flexible Working Time and Family Life: a Review of Changes.* London, Policy Studies Institute.

MESSICK D. M. and MACKIE D. M. (1989). 'Intergroup relations'. In M. R. Rosenzweig and L. W. Porter (eds), *Annual Review of Psychology*, 40, 45–81, Palo Alto, CA, Annual Reviews Inc.

MOLE J. (1990). *Mind Your Manners: Culture Clash in the Single European Market.* London, Industrial Society.

MORRISON E. W. and HERLIHY J. M. (1992). 'Becoming the best place to work: managing diversity at American Express travel related services', in Jackson S. E. and Associates (1992), 203–26.

MOTWANI J., HARPER E., SUBRAMANIAN R. and DOUGLAS C. (1993). 'Managing the diversified workforce: current efforts and future directions'. *SAM Advanced Management Journal*, 58, 3, 16–21.

NEDO (1990). *Women Managers: the Untapped Resource.* London, NEDO.

NEMETH C. J. (1986). 'Differential contributions of majority and minority influence'. *Psychological Review*, 93, 23–32.

NEW WAYS TO WORK (1993). *Change at the Top: Working Flexibly at Senior and Managerial Levels in Organisations.* London, New Ways to Work.

NKOMO S. M. (1992). 'The emperor has no clothes: rewriting "race in organizations" '. *Academy of Management Review*, 17, 3, 487–513.

PAINE L. S. (1994). 'Managing for organisational integrity'. *Harvard Business Review*, March–April, 72, 2, 106–17.

PAYNE J. (1991). *Women, Training and the Skills Shortage*. London, Policy Studies Institute.

PEARN M. A., KANDOLA R. S. and MOTTRAM R. D. (1987). *Selection Tests and Sex Bias: the Impact of Selection Testing on the Employment Opportunities of Women and Men*. London, HMSO.

PEDLER M., BURGOYNE J. and BOYDELL T. (1992). *The Learning Company*. Maidenhead, McGraw-Hill.

PENA N. E. (1992). 'Can equal opportunity be made more equal?' *Harvard Business Review*, March–April, 149.

PETTIGREW T. F. (1986). 'The intergroup contact hypothesis reconsidered'. In M. Hewstone and R Brown (eds), *Contact and Conflict in Intergroup Encounters*, Oxford, Basil Blackwell.

PHILLIPS N. (1992). Managing International Teams. London, Pitman Publishing.

POWELL G. N. (1988). *Women and Men in Management*. Newbury Park, CA, Sage.

POWELL G. N. (1990). 'One more time: Do female and male managers differ?' *Academy of Management Executive*, August, 68–76.

PROCTOR J. and JACKSON, C. (1992). *Women Managers in the NHS: a Celebration of Success*. London, NHS Management Executive.

RAJAN A. (1990). *1992: a Zero Sum Game: Business, know-how, and Training Challenges in an Integrated Europe*. London, Industrial Society.

RENNIE S. (1993). 'Equal opportunities as an ethical issue'. *Equal Opportunities Review*, September–October, 51, 56.

RIGG C. and SPARROW J. (1994). 'Gender, diversity and working styles'. *Women in Management Review*, 9, 1, 9–16.

ROBERTSON I. T. and KANDOLA R. S. (1982). 'Work sample tests: validity adverse impact and applicant reaction'. *Journal of Occupational Psychology*, 55, 171–83.

ROSENFIELD P., GIACALONE R. A. and RIORDAN, C. A. (1994). 'Impression management theory and diversity: lessons for organizational behaviour'. *American Behavioral Scientist*, 37, 5, 601–4.

ROSS R. and SCHNEIDER R. (1992). *From Diversity to Equality: a Business Case for Equal Opportunities*. London, Pitman Publishing.

ROSSETT A. and BICKHAM T. (1994). 'Diversity training: hope, faith and cynicism'. *Training*, 31, 1, 40–6.

SAAVEDRA R. (1990). 'Beer sales and delivery teams'. In J. R. Hackman (ed), *Groups that Work (and those that don't): Creating Conditions for Effective Teamwork*, San Francisco, CA, Jossey-Bass.

SCHMITT N. (1989). 'Fairness in employment selection'. In M. Smith and I. T. Robertson (eds), *Advances in Selection and Assessment*, Chichester, John Wiley.

SCHWARTZ F. N. (1992). 'Women as a business imperative'. *Harvard Business Review*, March–April, 105–14.

SENGE P. (1990). *The Fifth Discipline: the Art and Practice of the Learning Organisation*. New York, Doubleday.

SESSA V. I. (1992). Managing diversity at the Xerox Corporation: balanced workforce goals and caucus groups, in Jackson S. E. and Associates (1992), 37–64.

SHEPARD C. R. (1964). *Small Groups*. San Francisco, CA, Chandler Publishing.

SLY F. (1994). 'Ethnic groups and the labour market'. *Employment Gazette*, May, 147–60.

SMALL S. (1991). 'Attaining racial parity in the United States and England: we got to go where the greener grass grows!' *Sage Race Relations Abstracts*, May, 16, 2, 3–55.

STAEDELIN F. (1986). 'New forms of work organisation'. In *New Forms of Work and Activity*, The European Foundation for the Improvement of Living and Working Conditions.

STATA R. (1989). 'Organisational learning – the key to management innovation'. *Sloan Management Review*, Spring, 63–74.

STEPHAN C., PRESSER N., KENNEDY J. and ARONSON E. (1978). 'Attributions to success and failure in cooperative, competitive and interdependent interactions'. *European Journal of Social Psychology*, 8, 269–74.

STODGILL R. M. (1974). *Handbook of Leadership: a Survey of Theory and Research*. New York, Free Press.

STONEWALL (1993). *Less equal than others. A Survey of Lesbians and Gay Men at Work*. London, Stonewall.

STRAW J. (1989). *Equal Opportunities: the Way Ahead*. London, Institute of Personnel Management.

SYRETT M. and LAMMIMAN J. (1994). 'Developing the peripheral worker'. *Personnel Management*, July, 28–31.

TAJFEL H. (1970). 'Experiments in intergroup discrimination'. *Scientific American*, 223, 96–102.

THIEDERMAN S. (1994). 'Staff diversity: the best of all backgrounds'. *Association Management*, 46, 2, 57–60.

THOMAS D. A. and EVANS D. J. (1992). 'Can equal opportunity be made more equal?' *Harvard Business Review*, March–April, 156.

THOMAS R. R. (1990). 'From affirmative action to affirming diversity'. *Harvard Business Review*, March–April, 107–17.

THOMAS R. R. (1991). *Beyond Race and Gender: Unleashing the Power of Your Total Workforce by Managing Diversity*. New York, AMACOM.

THOMAS R. R. (1992). Managing diversity: a conceptual framework, in Jackson S. E. and Associates (1992), 306–18.

THOMAS V. C. (1994). 'The downside of diversity'. *Training and Development*, 48, 1, 60–62.

THOMPKINS N. (1992). 'Can equal opportunity be made more equal?' *Harvard Business Review*, March–April, 154.

TOWERS PERRIN/CBI (1992). *The Benefits Package of the Future: Survey Results October 1992*. London, Confederation of British Industry.

TRAINDIS H. C., HALL E. R. and McEWEN R. B. (1964). 'Member heterogeneity and dyadic creativity'. *Human Relations*, 18, 33–55.

TROMPENAARS F. (1993). *Riding the Waves of Culture: Understanding Cultural Diversity in Business*. London, Economist Books.

TROST C. (1990). 'Women managers quit not for family but to advance their corporate climb'. *Wall Street Journal*, 2 May.

VAUGHT B. C. and ABRAHAM Y. T. (1992). 'Cultural diversity and interpersonal communication skills: a study of Indian managers'. *Leadership and Organisation Development Journal*, 13, 7, 26–31.

WAINWRIGHT D. (1979). *Discrimination in Employment: a Guide to Equal Opportunity*. London, Associated Business Press.

WALKER B. A. and HANSON W. C. (1992). Valuing differences at Digital Equipment Corporation, in Jackson S. E. and Associates (1992), 119–37.

WARNER M. (1991). *Imagining a Democratic Culture*. London, Charter 88.

WATSON G. (1994). 'The flexible workforce and patterns of working hours in the UK'. *Employment Gazette*, July, 239–47.

WATSON W. E., KUMAR K. and MICHAELSEN L. K. (1993). 'Cultural diversity's impact on interaction process and performance: comparing homogeneous and diverse task groups'. *Academy of Management Journal*, 36, 3, 590–602.

WILDER D. A. (1986). 'Social categorisation: implications for creation and reduction of intergroup bias'. In L. Berkowitz (ed.), *Advances in Experimental Social Psychology*, 9, 291–355. New York, Academic Press.

WOO D. (1990). 'The "over-representation" of Asian Americans: red herrings and yellow perils'. *Sage Race Relations Abstracts*, May, 15, 2, 3–36.

WOOD R. (1994). 'Work sample should be used more (and will be)'. *International Journal of Selection and Assessment*, 2, 3, 166–71.

YOUNGBLOOD S. A. and CHAMBERS-COOK K. (1984) 'Child care assistance can improve employee attitudes and behaviour'. *Personnel Administrator*, February, 93–5.

Index

Appraisals, 126–30
  criteria for 126–7
  exclusive approach 129
  fairness 126–30
  improving process 128–9
  inclusive approach 129
  and training 127–8

Benefits mosaic 32–53
  access to talent 34, 37–40
  actual benefits 33–4
  available evidence 36
  categorisation of perceived benefits 35
  claimed benefits 33–4
  debatable benefits 35, 44–50
  defining heterogeneity 48–50
  evidence of retention 40
  flexibility of organisation 41–4
  improved customer service 45–6
  improved team effectiveness 46–50
  increased quality 44–5
  indirect benefits 35, 50–2
  links between diversity benefits 51–2
  perceived benefits 32–6
  proven benefits 35, 36–44
  reduced recruitment and associated costs 34
  reducing training costs 38
  research into team effectiveness 47

Demographic changes
  in Europe 30
  in UK 21–8
    age 24–5
    carers 26–7
    eldercare 26–7
    ethnic minorities 21–4
    National Economic Development Organisation Report (1990) 27–8
    people with disabilities 24
  women 25–6
  in USA 28–30
    age 29
    ethnic minorities 28–9
    females 29
    Hudson Institute 28
    immigration 29
Discrimination 9
  indirect 119–24
Diversity competence 102–15
Diversity initiatives 54–73
  least frequently implemented 57–9
  least likely to be assessed 64–5
  least successful 62–4
  monitoring 68–71
  most frequently implemented 56–7
  most likely to be assessed 65–6
  most successful 59–62
  priority areas for action 71–2
  reasons for taking action 66–8
  survey development 54–5
Diversity mosaic 6–20
Diversity-oriented organisation
  active flexibility 158–9
  aware workforce 155–8
  empowering culture 162–3
  fair process 154–5
  fair workforce 155–8
  individual focus 160–2
  and the learning organisation 104–72
  the learning organisation distinguished from 168–9
  mission 153–4
  'MOSAIC' 153
  objective process 154–5
  skilled workforce 155–8
  symbiotic model 169–71
  values of 153–4

Effective communication 88–91
Empowering culture 162–3

Equal opportunities 13–18
  age 16
  changing face of 13–18
  disability 15
  focus on business case 14
  gays and lesbians 15
  issues faced by other groups 14–15
  and managing diversity 173–4
Ethical conduct 16–18
  concern about 16–18
  corporate issue 17
  and sexual harassment 17–18
Ethnic minorities
  national picture 21–2
  regional patterns 22–3
European Union 30–1

Flexibility of organisation 41–4
France, and anti-discrimination
  legislation 18–19

Gaining diversity in processes 116–30
Globalisation of trade 30–1
Group membership, and individual
  needs 132–3

Heterogeneity 49–50

Improved team effectiveness 46–50
Increased quality 44–5
Individual
  communication style 113
  curiosity 112
  development 114
  examination of own behaviour 112
  flexibility 113–14
  honesty 113
  leadership 114
  role model 114–15
  role of 102–15
Induction 124–26
  improvement of processes 125–6
International Distillers and Vintners 12,
  98–101

Labour Force Survey 23
Learning organisation 164–72
  and the diversity-oriented

  organisation 164–72
  Pearn Kandola approach 165
  six-factor model 165–6
  symbiotic model 169–71
Legislation, mosaic of 18–19

Managing diversity
  and affirmative action 10–11
  benefits 174–5
  and competence 11
  concern for all employees 10
  culture of organisation 10
  definition of 6–13
  and discrimination 9
  and equal opportunities 11, 173–4
  factors 7–8
  individuals not groups 176
  meeting of business objectives 10
  movement within organisation 10
  new perspectives 175–6
  organisation as mosaic 8–9
  processes 176–7
  scope of 12–13
  systems 176–7
  working definition of 152–3
Minorities 102–4
Model for managing diversity 74–101
  accountability 88
  assessment of needs 83–5
  auditing needs 83–5
  average perceived success rating
    95–6
  clarity of objectives 85–7
  clear accountability 87–8
  communication with all staff 91
  content survey 94
  co-ordination of activity 91–2
  determining success rating 95–6
  effective communication 88–91
  evaluation 93
  formulation of policy 80
  hypothesis 94
  and organisational culture 84–5
  organisational vision 77–81
  process survey 95
  research stage 83
  sample items of communication 95
  strategic approach 74–6

strategy web 77
summary of results 97
testing hypothesis 96–7
top management commitment 81–2
training 90–1
validated 76–7
validation 93–7
Monolithic organisation 150–1
Multicultural organisation 150–1

Netherlands, and anti-discrimination
    legislation 18–19

Organisation of the future 150–72

Population mosaic 21–31
Positive action 131–49
    different views of 133–4
    diversity-oriented approach 141
    ethnic minorities 139–40
    implications in UK 137–41
    research on 135–7
    and stigma of incompetence 135–7
    and symptoms 140
    women 138–9
Plural organisation 150–1

Recruitment 116–18
    advertising in ethnic press 117

Selection 119–24
    development of new processes
        121–2, 123–4

and feedback 122
and piloting 122
techniques to optimise efficiency and
    fairness 120–1
Sexual harassment 17–18
Stereotyping 104–9
    and cultural differences 107
    dangers 106–7
    and education 109
    effects of 105–6
    gender 104
    key points 105
    meaning of 104
    race 105
    reinforcing of 107–9

Targets 131–49
    examples 146
    implications for 141–9
    and managers 145
    and opportunities 143–4
    poor setting of 142–3
    and systems 147
    tensions of group-centred approach
        145
    and tokenism 147–8
    unrealistic 142
Top management commitment 81–2
Training, and appraisal 127–8
Training costs 38

Universal benefit 131